Quilter's Pattern
Workbook

Quilter's Pattern Workbook

Creating Dramatically Different
Designs with Color

Kirstin Olsen

A Sterling/Main Street Book
Sterling Publishing Co., Inc.   New York

Library of Congress CIP Data Available

Designed by Ronald R. Misiur
Photographs by Ken White

10   9   8   7   6   5   4   3   2   1

A Sterling/Main Street Book

Published by Sterling Publishing Company, Inc.
387 Park Avenue South, New York, N.Y. 10016
Originally published as *Quilter's Color Workbook*
Text © 1990 by Kirstin Olsen
Illustrations © 1990 by Sterling Publishing Company, Inc.
Distributed in Canada by Sterling Publishing
% Canadian Manda Group, P.O. Box 920, Station U
Toronto, Ontario, Canada M8Z 5P9
Distributed in Great Britain and Europe by Cassell PLC
Villiers House, 41/47 Strand, London WC2N 5JE, England
Distributed in Australia by Capricorn Link Ltd.
P.O. Box 665, Lane Cove, NSW 2066
Printed and bound in Hong Kong
All rights reserved

Sterling ISBN 0-8069-0477-1

Contents

Preface

When I first began quilting, I was utterly confused. I had little previous experience with sewing, and I took up the hobby in the first place not because of love of crafts or fabric, but because of my interest in women's history. Over and over in college, as I studied the history and the writing of women in America, quilting surfaced as activity, practical skill, art form, and metaphor. I decided that something so central to the lives of so many women was worth exploring.

So I set out, with no experience, no knowledge, and no adequate tools, to make a quilt that included over 1,700 individual pieces. I bought a couple of quilting books (which turned out to be hopelessly uninformative), cut up some old clothes, and bought a little extra material, some needles, and some thread. I pieced during lectures and women's studies seminars, and, as long as I kept up with the discussions and my course work, my professors didn't seem to mind. The quilt got put aside from time to time as more pressing projects asserted themselves, but I always came back to it.

How I finished it, I will never know. I had no sewing machine, all the wrong needles, the wrong material, and no clue as to how to combine colors effectively. But somehow the quilt was completed, and in the end it was a pretty nice quilt; I still use it, and I love it dearly. Along the way, I developed enormous respect for the women who created beautiful bed covers. I also learned a great deal about quilting, through my own mistakes and a few much more helpful books that I acquired later. My subsequent quilting projects have been much easier, and much better organized.

Nevertheless, better information and a little practice alone could not solve one of my problems—color selection. It was difficult at first for me to envision how two or more colors would look together. Oh, sure, I could hold swatches together in the fabric store, but it was still hard to picture those fabrics on a grand scale. Picking the right colors took lots and lots and lots of practice.

It also meant spending a lot of money, sometimes on fabrics that I later found I couldn't use. And just as I'd decided on one color combination, I'd see a better one in a quilting book and be torn in two: should I go with my own choices or spend the money for new fabrics and try to match the colors in the book? I realized, finally, that there were simply too many possible variations on any pattern for anyone to imagine them all. The selection and arrangement of colors could even make the pattern look like another design altogether.

I decided that there were three ways for a beginner to start experimenting with color. She could plunge right in with her first group of fabrics and hope that the finished quilt looked attractive—trial and error on a large scale. She could spend more money, possibly much more, than was absolutely necessary and buy a large selection of fabrics, with expanded possibilities for success—an enjoyable but expensive method, and simply trial and error on a smaller scale. Or she could look at a book which showed her multiple color combinations for a number of quilt patterns, a book which could give her not one, but ten or twenty starting points for her imagination. That book did not exist when I first began quilting. All the books I could find showed one, two, or possibly three versions of each quilt pattern, and often the only photographs shown were in black-and-white. Many books gave next to no help with color selection and included only the patterns themselves, with few if any photographs. I decided, therefore, that I would write a book to help beginning quilters get over the hurdle of color selection, and the *Quilter's Pattern Workbook* is the result. (For more advanced quilters, the many and unusual design variations presented will prove valuable). Using my past experience and what seemed like mountains of sample fabrics, I've done some of the basic legwork that any quilter needs to select colors for a harmonious design. I've cut and pieced dozens of quilt blocks and reproduced their colors to show what marvelous variety there can be in many pieced patterns. I've also included basic quilting information and step-by-step instructions on constructing each of the patterns shown. I hope the book makes the creation of an original quilt a little easier.

Have fun!

I would like to thank several people whose assistance or advice was invaluable. Brian and Nancy, thank you for providing equipment which helped immensely in the preparation of this book; Eric and Leo, thank you for comments and suggestions; and Staci, thank you for your inexhaustible knowledge and patience.

Special thanks to Irwin Bear of P & B Fabrics in Burlingame, California, who generously provided all the fabrics illustrated in this book.

Introduction

The first rule in quilting, as in so many other things, is simple: whatever works is the right way to do it. Quilting techniques vary from person to person, and what suits the needs of one person may be awkward and uncomfortable for another. As long as the final product is durable and attractive, it is a success.

Following are some guidelines for choosing materials and colors and for constructing a quilt project. But remember—if one method is found that works better than another, that's the "right" way to do it.

QUILTING MATERIALS AND TOOLS

Fabric, Pattern, and Color

For beginning quilters, it's usually best to stick with the basics, and, in the case of fabrics, that means 100% cotton. It's traditional, easy to work with, and available in a wide variety of colors and patterns. If patterned fabrics are chosen, however, remember that special care must be taken when cutting the pieces and putting the quilt together. A square cut or sewn a bit askew is ten times more noticeable when the fabric is patterned. On the other hand, many beginners prefer patterned fabrics, since the eye is attracted to the design and not to the quilting stitches themselves, which on a first attempt may be a little shaky.

When selecting colors for quilt fabrics and designs, it is well to keep in mind some basic elements of color theory. There are three primary pigments—red, blue, and yellow—and three complementary colors—green, purple, and orange. Green is the complement of red, purple of yellow, and orange of blue. Adding black to these colors dims them; adding white brightens them.

Putting two colors adjacent to each other changes the nature of both, just as mixing them would. Primary red placed next to black will appear darker than the same red next to white. Also, putting red next to a similar color, like a red-orange, will have a blending effect. Putting the same red across from its complementary color, green, will make both colors appear truer and more distinct. This is because true red and true green have no common pigmentation that allows them to "blend," and this will be true of any primary-complementary color combination.

In addition, color choice can affect the impression of depth in a quilt pattern. Warmer colors—reds, oranges, yellows, and purples with a great deal of red in them—appear closer, while cool colors—blues, greens, and other purples—appear to recede from the viewer. Primary yellow seems the closest of all colors, while dark blue usually seems the farthest away. Of course, some blues seem closer or farther than others; this is due to mixtures of other colors (or black or white) in the dye. Generally speaking, darker colors will seem farther and lighter colors will seem nearer.

Finally, take into accout the responses people have to color. Scientific studies have shown that warmer colors, like primary yellow and red, tend to make people anxious and active. In a room dominated by these colors, people have trouble sitting still for long periods of

9

time. On the other hand, cool colors tend to soothe (as do earth tones, because of the association of them with natural surroundings). Therefore a quilt dominated by cool colors might be best used in a bedroom, and a wall hanging with a warmer color selection could be displayed elsewhere in the house.

The selection of colors and combinations thereof shown in these pages of designs varies widely from pattern to pattern. For example, the hexagon designs (see chapter 10) most graphically illustrate just how dramatically a basic pattern can change in appearance when different fabric colors are selected. And, of course, because of the placement of colors and the way in which they are perceived, a pattern can be "read" in two or three different ways. Illusionary effects are among the most intriguing and charming aspects of quiltmaking and, if studied and plotted carefully, can be easily reproduced.

One last pointer regarding color is to make certain that the fabrics selected are color fast. This is most easily done by simply dipping a swatch in warm water and squeezing the water out. A surprising amount of modern material does not have this essential quality.

After the color selection has been made, make sure that the fabric is the right weight—too heavy and it will be impossible to quilt, too light and it will be flimsy. Don't, for example, buy something that approaches denim or canvas in weight. Similarly, avoid fabrics so loosely woven that they're gauzy or somewhat transparent. When I first began quilting, I developed the habit of trying to read the price tag through a single layer of fabric; if I could come close, it was too thin for quilting.

Of course, not all quilters use 100% cotton. Some prefer cotton blends. However, if blends are to be used, make sure they're mostly cotton: 65% cotton, 35% polyester, for example. Furthermore, it's best to use the same type of fabric throughout a quilt. As experience is gained, several types of fabrics might be considered. A traditional pattern can be given an unusual flair when rendered in unexpected types of cloth.

Regular sewers are likely to have a variety of fabrics at their disposal. The most traditional, and I think the most enjoyable, fabrics for quilting are those salvaged from a family's old clothes. (Make sure the scraps are not so badly worn that they will no longer be durable.) Fabric that has been used often has a soft, mellow appearance, and its color has stood the test of time. A quilt top made completely or partially from old clothes is as nostalgic as a scrapbook or a photo album, and much more useful.

After the fabrics have been selected for the quilt top, purchase material which is similar in weight and color for the back of the quilt. Two or three pieces will probably be needed, especially if the quilt is very large. These are stitched together.

Most quilters prefer to prewash fabrics so that the cloth will not change shape later. Wash dark colors with dark colors, light colors with light colors. If the fabric has not been tested for its color fastness by this time, here is an opportunity to do so before it is too late. Running dye can ruin a quilt in which a lot of time and love has been invested, so err on the side of caution. After washing and drying the fabrics, iron them smooth. The pieces can not be cut properly if the cloth is wrinkled. Lastly, cut off the selvages—the edges of the cloth where the threads are woven very tightly to prevent raveling.

One final word of caution: always purchase a little more of each fabric than is thought needed. Make sure that all the pieces of a given type can be cut facing the same way along the grain of the fabric. Plenty of room is also needed for seam allowances. Plus, a decision may be made to revise a pattern a little, or some of the pieces may be misplaced or damaged—anything can happen. In particular, get plenty of backing fabric. It may be discovered that, although everything has been measured and cut and pieced carefully, the quilt top is somewhat larger than anticipated. If there is leftover fabric, it can be placed in the all-important scrap bag, or used to make matching pillows to go with the quilt. It's better to have too much than too little, especially when you are tying to match colors.

Needles

The needles used for quilting are called "betweens"—sizes #7, #8, and #9. Their small size allows the making of the tiny stitches so highly prized in hand quilting. These needles will seem abnormally small at first, and many quilters feel awkward using them. Try them out on a small test square first, just to get used to them.

Thread

The rule of thumb here—especially for beginners—is that the thread should match the cloth as closely as possible in color. Once experience is gained in making tiny, even stitches, this expertise can be displayed by choosing a contrasting color, but this must be done with care. It's easy, particularly if a quilt with a complex pattern is being made, for a contrasting thread color to make the whole project too distracting to the eye. Keep it simple until confidence is gained—and until the ego can handle the occasional failure.

There are several types of thread which are acceptable for use in quilts. A good rule is to match the piecing thread (the thread used to sew one piece of the quilt top to another) to the contents of the fabric being used. For example, if I'm using 100% cotton, I'll use cotton thread. If I'm using fabrics that are 65% cotton and 35% polyester, I may use cotton-covered polyester thread instead. There is also a variety of threads available for quilting. Unless shopping at a quilting store, however, probably only one type will be found—a specially coated cotton-covered polyester. It's a good, durable type of thread, and it comes in a fairly wide range of colors.

Some quilters prefer to coat their thread with beeswax before piecing or quilting. This makes the thread less likely to tangle and twist. If beeswax is used, slip the length of thread across the beeswax a couple of times.

A last note on the subject of thread: although it's tiresome to thread needle after needle, keep lengths of thread short! A piece of thread that is too long is more likely to tangle and fray. Use single, not double, threads, and keep them to about 18″ (45.7 cm) in length.

Batting

Both cotton-blend and 100% bonded polyester battings are widely available in quilting shops and fabric stores, and there is a variety of thicknesses. Bonded polyester battings require less actual quilting, since the structure of the batting itself keeps it from wandering or sagging too much. Cotton battings, on the other hand, give a quilt a more traditional look and feel. A thin layer of batting is easier to handle—a thick layer will give a quilt a fuller, puffier look. Be careful to choose a type of batting that achieves the look wanted and is not too frustrating to sew.

Other Quilting Tools

Thimbles are not necessary but helpful. Sore fingers can be most discouraging, and, once past the first stage of awkwardness, a thimble helps immensely. Rulers are indispensable. Clear plastic ones are best, and they're available not only at quilting shops but at most office or art supply stores.

Scissors should be sharp, high-quality, and never, never used to cut paper or cardboard.

Templates can be made out of cardboard or clear plastic. Clear plastic, of course, will be more durable.

Marking pens and pencils vary widely; I prefer a dressmaker's white pencil for dark fabrics and an easily washable marker, available at most fabric stores, for lighter colors. Do not, of course, use ordinary pens or markers, as these will not wash out.

Pins don't matter too much for piecing; as long as they're nice and sharp, they'll be fine. For quilting, however, there are long quilting pins available. These are better than short pins at holding together two layers of fabric and a layer of batting.

Quilting frames or hoops in some form are essential for quilting items larger than one or two blocks. I have a small apartment and limited funds, so in my case a quilting frame is out of the question. I tend to use large quilting hoops, which look like very sturdy embroidery hoops. Which method selected is entirely an individual choice—and, of course, if quilting on a sewing machine, neither a hoop nor a frame is needed.

Now that fabrics and colors have been selected and the necessary tools are in hand, step-by-step directions for assembling any of the fifteen projects shown in this book—and their over one hundred design variations illustrated in color—can begin.

MARKING AND CUTTING THE FABRIC

The first step in marking the fabric is to transfer the necessary pattern pieces from this book to the template material. Most of the pattern pieces are shown full size; a few are so large that they are drawn one-half or one-quarter actual size, and these will require enlarging before a template can be created. Everyone has her own way of copying the patterns. If transparent plastic sheets are being used, it's easy. Just place the sheet over the pattern in the book or the sheet on which you have enlarged it, tape it in place so it can't jiggle, and trace the pattern onto the plastic. Use a ruler, and do the tracing looking straight down at the pattern. This is done so that the pattern will be as little distorted as possible. A good way to do it is to place the pattern and plastic at the edge of a table and to stand, not sit, at the table.

Another method is particularly appropriate for cardboard templates. Place the cardboard beneath the page or sheet with the pattern on it and place a sheet of carbon paper or dressmaker's pattern paper between the pattern and the cardboard with the carbon side facing the cardboard. Making sure that the pattern, carbon paper, and cardboard will not move, trace the design. Then carefully cut out the template. If a relatively thick cardboard is being used, consider cutting it with an X-Acto knife to reduce distortion or bending of the template.

If no carbon paper is available, tracing paper or thin typing paper can be used to trace the design. Then cut out the tracing and paste it carefully to the cardboard.

Photocopying the pattern and mounting it on cardboard is not recommended as photocopying machines alter angles slightly.

Once the templates are ready, lay out one of the pieces of the fabric, placing the horizontal and vertical lines of the template along the straight grain and any diagonal lines or curves along the bias. Draw around the edge of the template, being careful not to pull on the fabric or make it pucker. Try to point the tip of the marking pen or pencil inward, toward the template. Otherwise, the line you draw may be farther away from the template on one side or the other, and the pattern piece will be slightly irregular.

Make each pattern piece of the same type in exactly the same orientation—same sides along the straight grain, same sides along the bias. If some pieces are marked and cut in the wrong orientation, it will show, especially if the fabric is a print rather than a solid color.

Most quilt books recommend leaving a ¼″ (6 mm) seam allowance on each pattern piece. If this is to be the guideline, make sure to leave about ½″ (13 mm) between pattern pieces as they are marked; then cut along the middle of the margin. Personally, I think it's easier to handle the pieces if there's a little extra width in the seam allowance.

ASSEMBLING THE QUILT BLOCK

When all seam lines are marked on the wrong side of the fabric and all of the individual quilt pieces are cut and ready to go, piecing the quilt top can begin. The basic unit of the top is the block—one repetition of the design. Specific piecing instructions are included with each pattern shown in this book, but here are a few tips that apply to all pieced quilts.

Pieces get sewn with their right sides facing each other so that the seam allowance faces the bottom, or wrong, side of the fabric. Place the pieces to be joined with their right sides facing each other, and match up the appropriate seam lines on each piece. Push a pin through the beginning and end points of the seam line. This not only holds the pieces together during sewing, but also insures that the seam lines are perfectly aligned before beginning sewing. Push another pin through the middle of the seam line, making sure that it pierces the middle of the seam line on the other piece. If the seam line is fairly long, add more pins, making sure not to bunch the fabric on either side. I like to have a pin in place every couple of inches.

Now that the pieces are pinned together, sew along the seam line with small straight stitches. In many cases, stitches can be begun and ended in the seam allowance itself. Do not sew into the seam allowance on points and triangles. If this is done, later pieces will be practically impossible to add, and seams will have to be resewn. Add any appliqué pieces last. Pin them in place with their seam allowances folded under and blindstitch them to the block. For curved pieces, cuts in the seam allowance will be needed almost to the seam line, at regular intervals.

Note: I prefer to press my seams open when piecing. A good many quilters, however, prefer to press seams to one side after piecing, primarily because of the difference in the way the fabric lies. I have also been known to use this technique on occasion, especially when working with very light-colored fabrics. Pressing the seams away from the light fabric keeps the seam allowance from showing through. In the individual project instructions that follow, I have advised that the seams be pressed open, but they can be pressed to the side if that is preferred.

ASSEMBLING THE ENTIRE QUILT

Yes, there are ways to quilt each block separately and then to join them all together at the end—but they're just as complicated, if not more so, than simply doing it all at once. Quilting the whole bedcover does take a good bit of room, but so do the last stages of joining the individual blocks. Furthermore, quilting it all at once means fewer sheets of bonded batting can be used, which I find to be easier. And, to be perfectly honest, I find it more psychologically satisfying to work on the whole quilt.

To assemble a quilt, you need three things—batting cut to size, backing cut to size, and the completed quilt top. The size of the quilt—and thus the size of the batting—should be determined by a measurement of the bed on which the quilt is intended to be used. Measure not only the top of the bed, but the sides as well—to the floor, or to whatever height thought appropriate. Remember to leave a little extra near the pillows if the quilt is to be tucked under them a bit. The size of the top and backing may be affected by how the quilt is to be bound (see "Binding the Quilt"). To make the quilt back, use extra-wide fabric or two or three lengths of fabric sewn together horizontally. If more than one piece of fabric is being used for the quilt back, take seam allowances into account when estimating fabric needs.

Completing the quilt top is just an extension of piecing the individual blocks; those blocks are simply pieced together, with or without a sash or neutral border between them. Whether or not a sash is used depends on the design and on individual preference. How wide the sash is made is also optional. (Sometimes the horizontal and vertical sashes must be of different widths, if only at the outside borders. In this case, the "B" pieces described in the following example will be rectangles, not squares, and special care must be used to assemble the pieces in the correct order.)

To assemble a quilt top without a sash, simply piece the blocks together in rows, and then piece the rows together. To assemble a quilt top with a sash, cut strips as long as the quilt blocks and as wide as desired (with, of course, a seam allowance of at least ¼″ [6 mm]). We'll call these the "A" strips. Now, cut squares from the sash fabric which are as long on each side as the "A" strips are wide. We'll call these the "B" squares. Piece horizontal rows together just as one would for a quilt without a sash. The top row will consist of alternating "B" squares and "A" strips, with the strips lying horizontally. The next row will consist of alternating "A" strips and quilt blocks, with the "A" strips standing vertically. The next row will look just like the top row, and so on. When all of the horizontal rows are pieced, join them together so the blocks are surrounded on all sides by the sash material.

When the quilt top, batting, and backing are ready, pin them together with the right sides of the fabric facing outward. Baste the entire quilt together, starting from the center and working toward the edges. This loose stitching will hold the three layers together while quilting. The thread used for basting should be of a color that contrasts with the colors in the top and backing: the basting stitches will be removed when the quilting is done, and the stitches must be easy to see.

Now quilting can be begin. The quilting pattern used may follow the design of the quilt top, or it may not. Following the design, or outline quilting, is preferred by many beginning quilters because it is relatively easy and almost certain to be harmonious with the pattern of the quilt top. However, especially in sash areas, a different quilting pattern may be desirable. Floral and leaf patterns are quite common as are geometric shapes and interlocking curves. Many books include quilting patterns, though copying patterns used on antique quilts or inventing designs can often be more enjoyable and rewarding than using ones in books.

Mark the quilting pattern or patterns much as was done with the pieces of the quilt top—with an easily removable marking pen or pencil. Take tiny, even stitches—the tinier the better. Start each length of thread by tying a knot and pulling the knot through the backing and into the batting, but not all the way through. When coming close to the end of the thread after quilting for a while, tie a knot in the thread near the fabric and do the same thing—pull the knot through one layer of fabric and into the batting, but not out the other side. Then clip the thread close to the fabric.

Sewing machines can be useful for quilting. A machine can sew a number of different and often very interesting stitches, and these stitches can almost always be as small as desired, but the sewing machine doesn't have the infinite versatility of hand sewing, so make machine-sewn quilting patterns relatively simple. Quilt from the center outward.

BINDING THE QUILT

The easiest way to bind a quilt (but not necessarily the best) is to self-bind or self-finish it. To self-bind the quilt, allow a little extra fabric on the quilt top or back. When quilting is complete, fold the excess over the raw edge, turn under the edge of the binding, and stitch it down. The obvious advantage of self-binding is that it's easy. The disadvantage is that the edges of a quilt tend to get the most wear, and it's often best to use a binding that can be removed.

Separate bindings are generally ½″ (13 mm) to 2″ (5.1 cm) wide, and there are two basic theories as to their construction. In both cases, the binding is cut on the bias—which means that several pieces will have to be sewn together along the diagonal. Some stores carry continuous bias binding, but make sure it's made of good quality material.

In the first method of bias binding, the binding is cut four times wider than the desired width—that is, if 1½″ (3.8 cm) of binding is wanted to show on the front of the quilt, the binding must be cut 6″ (15.2 cm) wide. Fold the binding in half, wrong sides together, and press. Open the fold, fold the edges of the strip toward the center, and press the two new folds. Place the binding around the raw edges of the quilt with the center crease forming the outer edge. Pin in place with the edges still folded under. Sew the binding on with an unobtrusive stitch.

In the second method of bias binding, the binding is cut only about ½″ (13 mm) wider than the desired width. Fold the binding in half, wrong sides together. Press. Line up the fabric edges with the top raw edge of the quilt, with the pressed and folded edge facing the center of the quilt. Sew the raw binding edges to the raw quilt edge, about ¼″ (6 mm) away from the edge. Fold the pressed and folded edge to the back side of the quilt and blindstitch to the back, thus covering the raw edges.

Corners may be finished in a number of ways. Bias binding can be broken into four separate strips, one for each side of the quilt: overlap the edges at the four corners. Corners can be mitered by gathering the excess fabric at the corners and folding it under itself to form a diagonal line. The stretchability of the bias-cut fabric can be used to "ease" the fabric around the corner without mitering it at all. The choice is an individual one.

CARING FOR THE FINISHED QUILT

So now the quilt is finished. The only task left is to keep its colors vibrant and its construction strong. Keep the quilt out of direct sunlight, which will fade it. Dust it periodically by shaking it vigorously but not carelessly. Let it rest periodically—use it for a few months, then give its fibers a break. In theory, it shouldn't need washing more than once a year.

Dry cleaning is not as efficient as washing for quilts, although antique quilts are a special case requiring very careful cleaning. New quilts should be carefully machine or hand washed. If a quilt is to be machine washed, use a very mild soap, and make sure that the soap is thoroughly dissolved in the water before the quilt is put in the machine. Use a delicate cycle and warm water—never hot. And, for heaven's sake, don't use bleach. Hand washing is gentler on the quilt, but far more work. Fill a clean bathtub with warm water and carefully stir the quilt with your hands. Again, use a mild detergent. Do not wring the quilt.

Ideally, quilts should be line-dried or spread out where lots of air (but not harsh sunlight) can get to them. They may, however, be put in a dryer on the coolest possible setting and taken out before they are totally dry.

Store quilts in a cool dark place. They should be rolled, not folded, but if there is no other choice than to fold them, remove them periodically and refold them in a different way. Quilts which remain folded in the same way for too long develop permanent creases. Do not wrap the quilt in plastic; let it breathe. Wrap it in a sheet or a piece of cotton. With care and attention, the quilts will serve well for years and years.

Quilter's Pattern Workbook

1.
Pinwheel

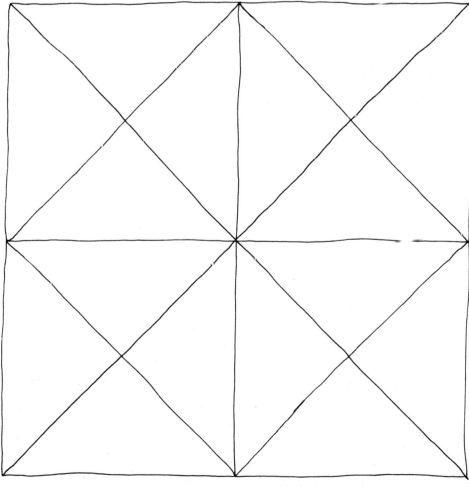

Also known as Windmill, this bold, simple pattern uses only sixteen pieces in each block — all of which are triangles. By using color in different combinations, the pattern can be rendered in a number of imaginative ways that will intrigue even the advanced quilter.

Piecing Instructions

1. Measure the bed for which the quilt is intended, as described in the Introduction. Decide whether or not sashes will be used between the Pinwheel blocks; Pinwheel is ideal for use with sashes. Next, calculate the number of blocks needed. Each block is a 12″ (30.5 cm) square, so with sashes of moderate width at least four blocks will be required for a crib quilt, twenty-four for a twin-size bed, and thirty for a full, queen, or king-size bed. If especially wide or narrow sashes are used, no sashes at all, or if the bed is an unusual size, the number of blocks will, of course, vary. It may also be necessary to adjust the size of the quilt slightly so that the sashes running around the edges of the quilt can be of the same width; sometimes the numbers don't come out quite right, and too much horizontal or vertical space is left over. Each 12″ (30.5 cm) Pinwheel block of sixteen triangles requires at least ⅓ to ½ yard (30.5 to 45.7 cm) of fabric.

2. Cut all pattern pieces, lining up the arrows on the pattern with the straight grain of the fabric and leaving seam allowances of at least ¼″ (6 mm).

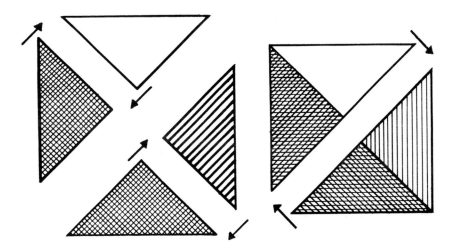

3. Attach the triangles in groups of four to form squares; first sew eight pairs of triangles, then join the pairs to form squares. Open and press seams. Make sure the points are lined up extra carefully when pinning prior to sewing since it's easy to make small errors which become obvious later on. Also, make sure triangles of the correct colors are joined together. Avoid having to undo the work because, for example, a black square was mistakenly put where a white one should be.

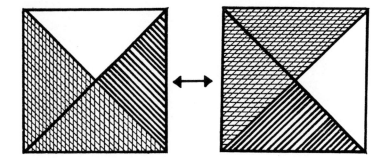

4. Sew the four individual squares into two pairs of squares; open and press seams.

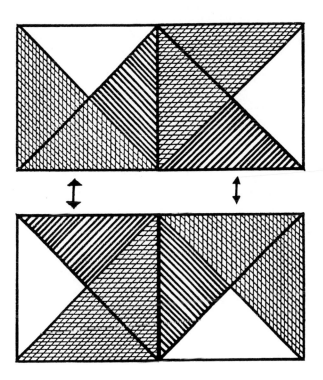

5. Sew the two pairs of squares together; open and press seams. A complete Pinwheel block is now in hand.

6. Repeat steps 3 through 5 until the appropriate number of blocks have been completed. Finish the project as outlined in the Introduction.

Pattern Piece

Shown full size

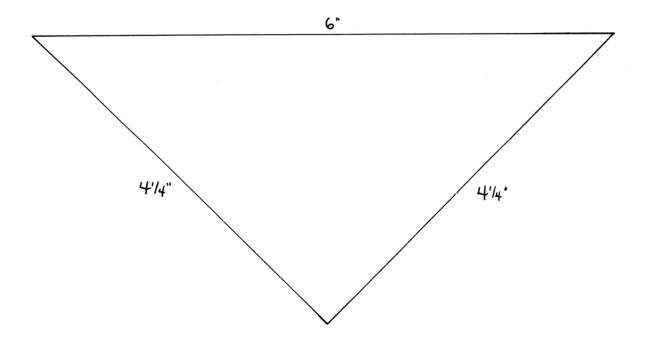

The classic treatment of the Pin-wheel or Windmill pattern is portrayed in the photograph on page 18, but this pattern offers a number of other possibilities shown on the opposite page. A smaller windmill can be created as in numbers 1 and 2, or a double pinwheel as in design 3. Designs 4 through 9 present a series of triangles and/or diamonds. A mirror-image crown is created in design 10, a basket-weave effect in 11, and a bold chevron in 12.

2.
Ohio Star

This pattern is known by a bewildering variety of names, but its most common designations are Ohio Star, Variable Star, and Amish Star. As you might have guessed from the last name listed, it's a very popular pattern among Amish quilters. The basic block is made up of twenty-one pieces—five squares and sixteen triangles.

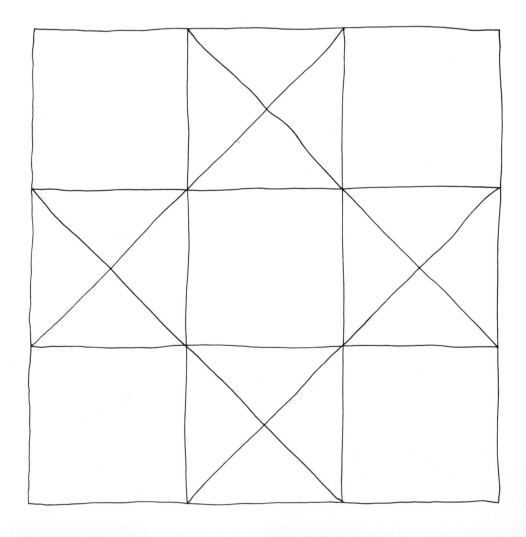

Piecing Instructions

1. Measure the bed for which the quilt is intended, as described in the Introduction. Decide whether sashes will be used between the Ohio Star blocks and how wide they will be; sashes, especially wide sashes, make the most of the simple beauty of this pattern. Next, calculate how many blocks are needed. Each block is 12″ (30.5 cm) square, so with sashes of moderate width at least four blocks will be needed for a crib quilt, twenty-four blocks for a twin-size bed, and thirty blocks for a full, queen, or king-size bed. If especially wide or narrow sashes are used, no sashes at all, or if the bed is of an unusual size, the number of blocks will of course vary. It may be necessary to adjust the size of the quilt slightly so that the sashes running around the edges of the quilt can be of the same width since the numbers don't always come out quite right and too much horizontal or vertical space is left. Each Ohio Star block of twenty-one pieces requires ¼ yard (22.9 cm) of fabric.

2. Cut all the pattern pieces, lining up the arrows on the pattern with the straight grain of the fabric. Leave seam allowances of at least ¼″ (6 mm)

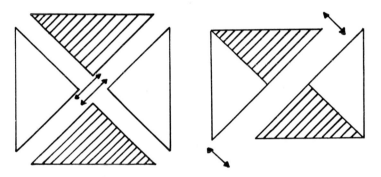

3. Construct the four "points" of the star by using four triangles to make a square. First sew the triangles into pairs; open and press seams. Then join the pairs to form squares; open and press seams.

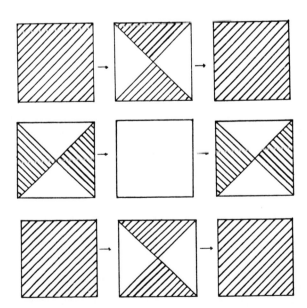

4. Piece three horizontal rows. The top row will have a plain square, a composite square made of four triangles, and then another plain square. The

Drawings 1 and 2 (opposite) represent the two most common versions of this pattern. The finished quilt block in the photograph reverses the positioning of light and dark fabrics seen in drawing 1, and emphasizes how different effects are achieved by the placement of color. Number 3 is, depending on your perspective, a two-toned star on a light-colored background or a star just like that in number 1, with an inner diamond. In drawings 4 and 5 the central square becomes part of the background and four squares made up of triangles emerge. In each block, however, the composition of the squares is different. In 6, making one-half of every other square the same color as the background creates a striking pinwheel. This variation is particularly well-suited to unsashed quilts as the triangles join at the sides of the squares to form parallelograms. Number 7 creates a four-pointed rather than an eight-pointed star. Number 8 creates a large X; this is another variation that works well without sashes. A central diamond is added in 9 to the four triangles on the sides of the block. Used without sashes, it creates an intriguing network of X's and diamonds. Number 10 uses a simple cross formation. Number 11 has a strong vertical look, and 12 is a completely different approach to this design, turning the star and diamonds into arrows pointing in all directions.

middle row should have a composite square, a plain square, and then another composite square. The bottom row should have a plain square, a composite square, and then a plain square. Open and press seams.

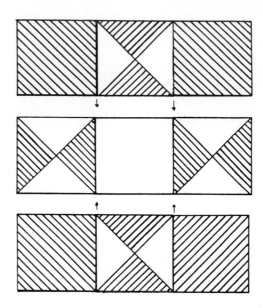

5. Attach the top row to one side of the middle row and the bottom row to the other side of the middle row. Open and press seams.

6. One Ohio Star block is now finished. Repeat steps 3 through 5 until all the blocks needed are completed. Finish the quilt as directed in the Introduction.

Pattern
Pieces

Shown full size

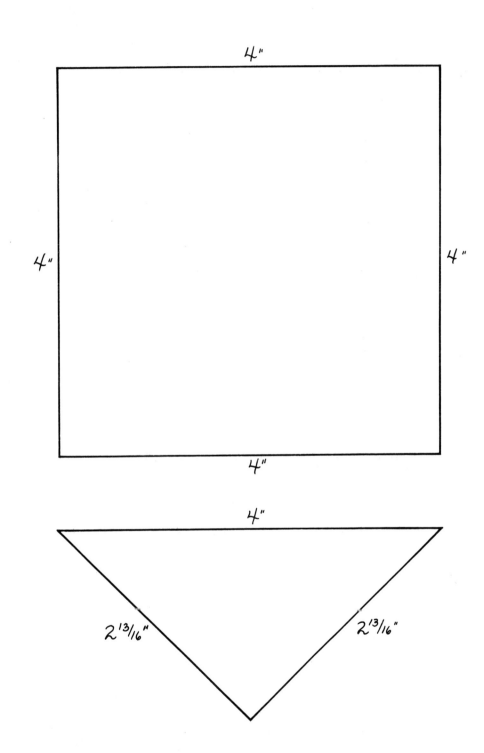

3.
Chimney Sweep

This is a very easy pattern, although it may not appear so at first. Think of it in terms of diagonal rows. From the top left, the first row is a triangle; the second, a triangle, a square, and a triangle; and so on. Altogether there are forty-one pieces — twenty-five squares, twelve large triangles, and four small triangles.

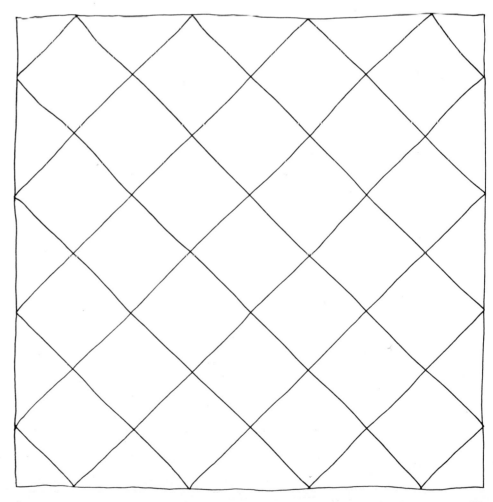

Piecing Instructions

1. Measure the bed for which the quilt is intended, as described in the Introduction. Decide whether sashes will be used between the Chimney Sweep blocks and how wide they are to be. (I prefer this pattern with a sash). Next, calculate how many blocks are needed. Each block is 12″ (30.5 cm) square, so with a sash of moderate width at least four blocks will be needed for a crib quilt, twenty-four blocks for a twin-size bed, and thirty blocks for a full, queen, or king-size bed. If especially wide or narrow sashes are used, no sashes at all, or if the bed is an unusual size, the number of blocks will of course vary. It may be necessary to adjust the size of the quilt so that the sashes running around the edges of the quilt can be of the same width, since the numbers don't always come out quite right and too much horizontal or vertical space is left. Each block of forty-one pieces will require at least ⅓ yard (30.5 cm) of fabric.

2. Cut all pattern pieces, lining up the arrows on the pattern with the straight grain of the fabric and leaving seam allowances of at least ¼″ (6 mm).

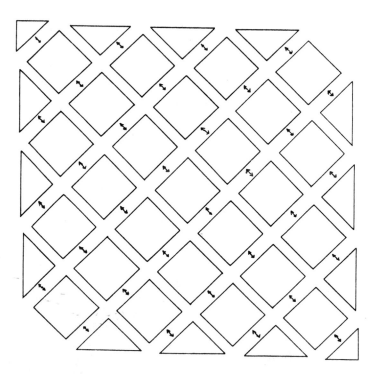

3. Sew each of the diagonal rows by piecing squares and triangles together. Open and press seams.

The endless variety of Chimney Sweep is only hinted here. The quilt block in the photograph on page 30 illustrates one of the basic variations in which a centrally placed X is outlined in contrasting fabric. Depending on the positioning of light and dark fabrics, the design takes on a different look (see opposite page). Numbers 1, 2, and 3 are variations of the design in the photograph. Other options include individual diamonds as in 4, and a variety of Xs as in 5 and 6. The many other motifs which can be created with the Chimney Sweep pattern include chevrons as in 7; jagged horizontal rows, shown in 8; concentric diamonds, 9; irregular shapes, 10; and basket-weave effects, 11 and 12.

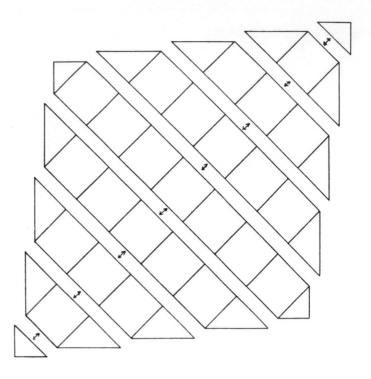

4. Line up and join the diagonal rows to form a square. Open and press each seam. The Chimney Sweep block is now complete. Attach the number of blocks required and sashes (if any), and finish the quilt as outlined in the Introduction.

Note: One optional method of piecing the quilt is to use the large triangle pattern marked "optional," illustrated with the other pattern pieces. Cut four large pieces of fabric for each Chimney Sweep block. Sew one to each side of each block. This creates larger squares and allows the pattern to be rotated 45 degrees.

Pattern Pieces

Shown full size

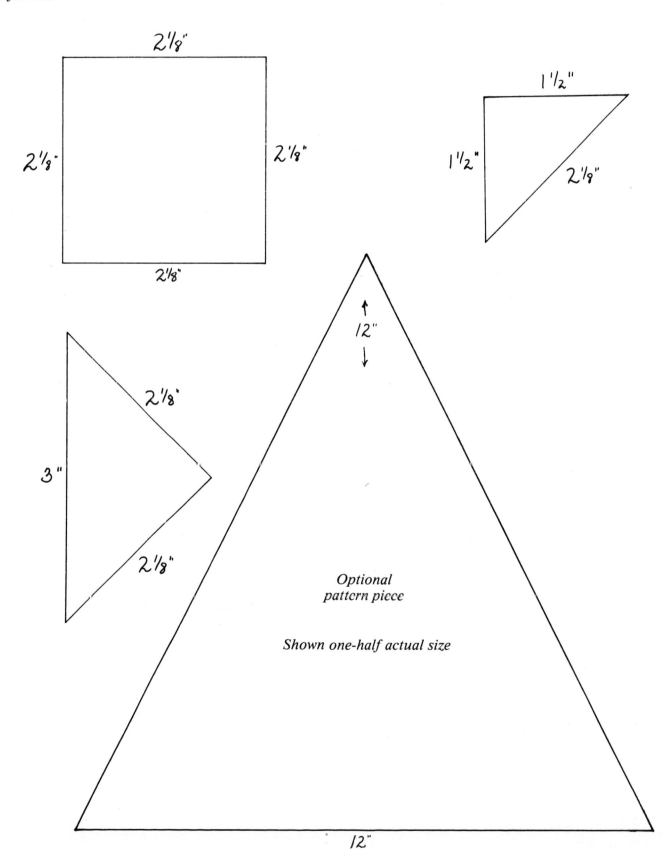

2¹⁄₈"

2¹⁄₈"

2¹⁄₈"

2¹⁄₈"

1¹⁄₂"

1¹⁄₂"

2¹⁄₈"

3"

2¹⁄₈"

2¹⁄₈"

12"

12"

*Optional
pattern piece*

Shown one-half actual size

4.
Mosaic

A dramatic pattern with practically unlimited possibilities, Mosaic is actually quite simple to piece. Only thirty-two pieces are called for, all of which are the same triangular form.

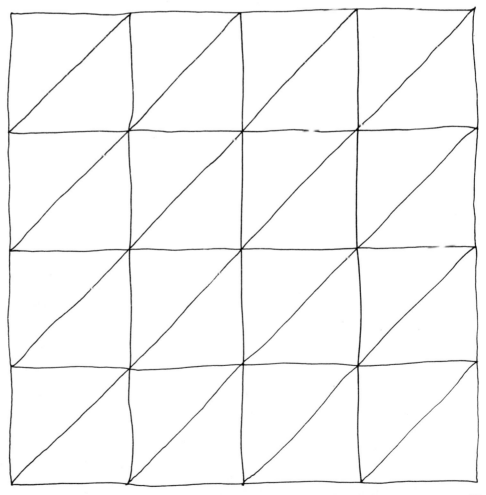

Piecing Instructions

1. Measure the bed for which the quilt is intended, as described in the Introduction. Decide whether sashes will be used between the Mosaic blocks and how wide they will be. Next, calculate how many blocks are needed. Each block is 12″ (30.5 cm) square, so with sashes of moderate width, at least four blocks will be needed for a crib quilt, twenty-four blocks for a twin-size bed, and thirty blocks for a full, queen, or king-size bed. If especially wide or narrow sashes are used, no sashes at all, or if the bed is an unusual size, the number of blocks will of course vary. It may be necessary to adjust the size of the quilt slightly so that the sashes running around the edges can be the same width since the numbers don't always come out quite right and too much horizontal or vertical space is left over. Each thirty-two-piece Mosaic block requires ¼ yard (22.9 cm) of fabric.

2. Cut all of the basic pattern pieces, lining up the arrows on the pattern with the straight grain of the fabric and leaving seam allowances of at least ¼″ (6 mm).

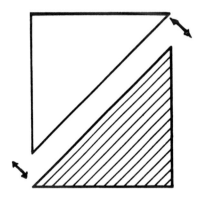

3. The way to piece Mosaic is to think of it not as thirty-two triangles, but as four rows of four squares each. The squares merely happen to be made of two triangles each. Keeping this in mind, attach pairs of triangles so that they make squares. Be especially careful when pinning the pieces together; it's easy to get the points a little bit askew if you're not diligent. Also, be careful to match the correct triangles! The chosen color scheme will look a little odd if the pieces have been mismatched! To avoid confusion, work in a specific order—for example, from left to right and from top to bottom.

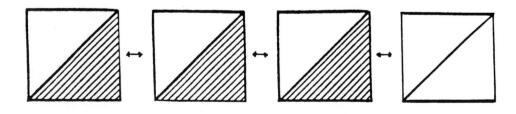

4. Construct the top row by sewing the appropriate four squares together. Sew the first square to the second and the third to the fourth, and then join the two pairs. Open and press seams.

5. Repeat step 4 for the other three rows.

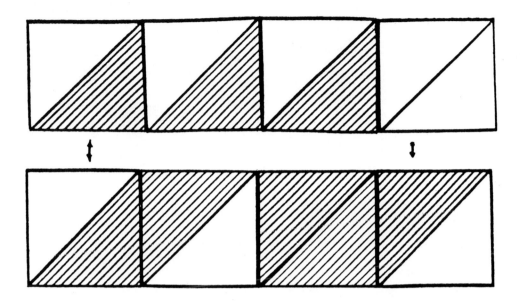

6. Attach the top row to the second row, and the third row to the bottom row. Open and press seams.

7. Attach the top to the second row, and the third row to the bottom row. Open and press seams.

8. Repeat steps 3 through 7 until as many blocks are completed as needed. Finish the quilt as directed in the Introduction.

Pattern
Piece

Shown full size

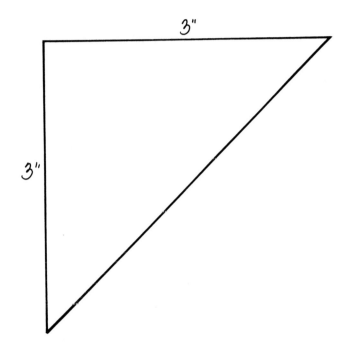

A variety of elements can be seen within the Mosaic pattern. The quilts in the photograph on page 36 and in drawings 1 through 3 (on opposite page) emphasize the basic design—a set of triangles facing each other to form a sort of feathered diagonal shape. In some of these drawings the feathered shape is hollow; in some it's solid. In others it's more obvious; in others, less so. Numbers 4 and 5 bring out different shapes in the design—parallelograms or slanted hexagons. Number 6 is a series of jagged lines. Number 7 emphasizes the sixteen squares in the block, each of which is split into a light and a dark half. Sixteen squares make up 8 and 9, but in 8 the squares are solid, and in 9 one-half of each square is green, creating the impression of many colored triangles against a solid background. Block 10 is a constantly shifting variation: at one moment the dark green triangles stand out, then the yellow triangles and parallelograms become prominent, and finally diagonal lines or horizontal bars appear. Numbers 11 and 12 are more clear-cut, combining bold, broad bands of color with two-toned squares in which the triangles rather than the squares are predominant.

5.
Triangles

Used with or without sashes, Triangles can be a bold, versatile, dynamic, and fascinating pattern. There's only one catch: extreme care must be taken when joining the rows, lest the points of the triangles not line up properly. The pattern is composed of 120 whole equilateral triangles (3" or 7.6 cm on each side) and 16 half-triangles.

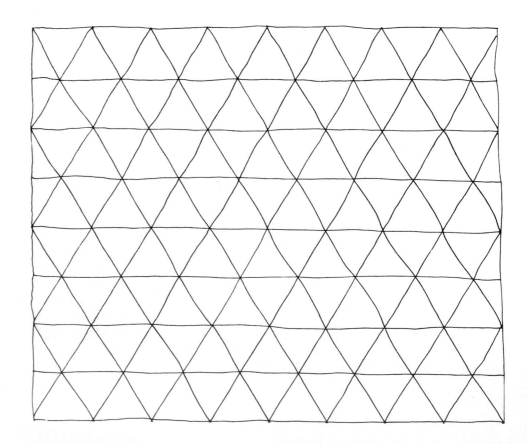

Piecing Instructions

1. Measure the bed for which the quilt is intended, as described in the Introduction. The area in the photographed example measures approximately 24″ wide (61 cm) by 20″ (50.8 cm) long. If the block is to be used without sashes, and annoying lines running through the middle of some of the triangles are not wanted, a little math will be needed to determine how many of the half triangles will become whole triangles in the process of joining blocks.

   A little math is also required to figure out how many blocks (and, perhaps, partial blocks) will be needed. When it is determined how large the quilt is to be, figure out the maximum number of blocks that will fit entirely within those boundaries, horizontally and vertically. Then take the inches or centimetres left over in each dimension (if there are any) and decide what should be done: (1) shorten the quilt by that much, (2) add another whole block to each side and make the quilt larger than intended, or (3) use only as much of the block as needed.

   The third option is the most satisfying solution, but also the most difficult to achieve. Fortunately, Triangles lends itself fairly well to this sort of adaptation. Vertical distance is easy to add in small increments, since the pattern separates itself into horizontal rows. And since the base of each triangle is 3″ (7.6 cm) long (and the base of each half-triangle, therefore, 1½″ or 3.8 cm), the horizontal distance can be extended in increments of 1½″ (3.8 cm) without needing different pattern pieces. Each block of Triangles requires ⅔ to ¾ yard (61 cm to 68.6 cm) of fabric.

2. Cut all of the pattern pieces, lining up the arrows on the pattern with the straight grain of the fabric and leaving seam allowances of at least ¼″ (6 mm).

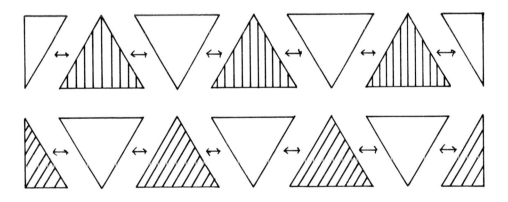

3. Sew the triangles together in horizontal rows, opening and pressing seams as you go along. Be careful to get the colors in the right order; keep a diagram in front of you until the pattern is known backwards and forwards by rote. Since all the pieces look the same in Triangles, it's easy to get confused.

In the quilt in the photograph above each triangle is distinct from the other.
This is not so in drawings 1 and 2 opposite, where the triangles join together to
form diagonal bands. In 1 the color shifts are soft and gradual; in 2 the bands
are quite sharp and distinct, with a thorny appearance. Numbers 3 through 7
bring out some of the diamonds hidden in the pattern. The Southwestern motif
and soft pastels in 8, and the arrowhead motif of 9, are particularly unusual
variations, as is the jagged, spidery bolt of lightning seen in 10. More typical are
11, with its simple hexagons and diamonds, and 12, made up of six-pointed
stars. Notice how the star pattern appears quite distinct from the quilt surface.
This is accomplished by using a variety of colors for each point. When the stars
done in a two-color scheme they appear more fla

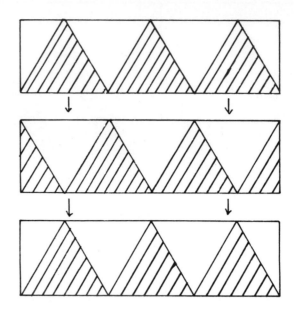

4. Sew the horizontal rows together to form the quilt top. Be especially careful when pinning these rows. It's very difficult at first to get the points of the triangles to line up. Open and press seams.

5. Finish the quilt as outlined in the Introduction.

Pattern Pieces

Shown full size

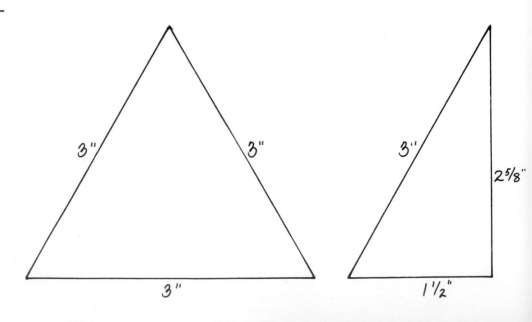

6.
Wrench

Also known as Monkey Wrench, Hole in the Barn Door, and Churn Dash, Wrench is a classic pattern found in Amish and Mennonite quilts. Only twenty-one pieces of four basic forms are required for each block—eight triangles, one square, four wide rectangles, and eight narrow rectangles.

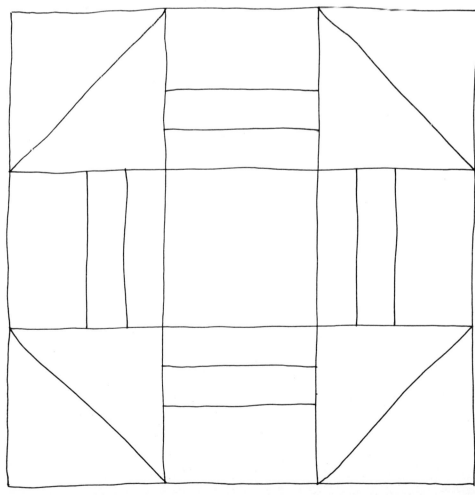

Piecing Instructions

1. Measure the bed for which the quilt is intended, as described in the Introduction. Decide whether or not sashes will be used between the Wrench blocks and how wide they will be. The pattern is quite suitable for quilts with or without sashes. Next, calculate how many blocks will be needed. Each block is a 12″ (30.5 cm) square, so with sashes of moderate width at least four blocks will be needed for a crib quilt, twenty-four for a twin-size bed, and thirty for a full, queen, or king-size bed. If especially wide or narrow sashes are used, no sashes at all, or if the bed is an unusual size, the number of blocks will of course vary. It may be necessary to adjust the size of the quilt so that the sashes running around the edges of the quilt can be the same width since the numbers don't always come out quite right and too much horizontal or vertical space is left.

   Each 12″ (30.5 cm) block requires at least ¼ yard (22.9 cm) of fabric and is made up of eight triangles, one square, four wide rectangles, and eight narrow rectangles.

2. Cut all of the pattern pieces, lining up the arrows on the pattern with the straight grain of the fabric and leaving seam allowances of at least ¼″ (6 mm).

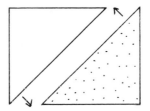

3. Wrench is basically composed of three rows of three squares each. One square is a plain 4″ (10.2 cm) square; four are composed of two triangles each; and four are composed of three rectangles, one wide and two narrow. First construct four squares by sewing the eight triangles together. Be especially careful when pinning and sewing these; it's hard to get points to match up perfectly. Open and press seams.

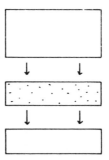

4. Next construct the four squares that are made up of rectangles. To make each square, sew two narrow rectangles together along their long sides. Then sew a wide rectangle to a pair of narrow rectangles. Open and press seams.

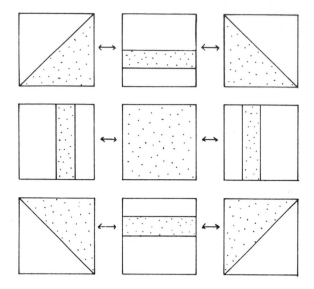

5. There should now be nine squares of equal size: one plain, four made of triangles, and four made of rectangles. Sew them into three horizontal rows. The top row will have a triangle-square, then a rectangle-square (with the rectangles lying horizontally), and then another triangle-square. The middle row will have a rectangle-square with the rectangles standing vertically, then the plain square, and then another rectangle-square with the rectangles standing vertically. The bottom row should be pieced in the same order as the top row.

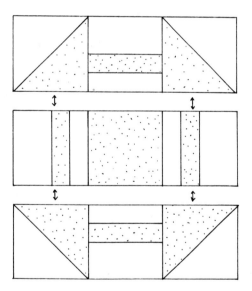

6. Sew the top and bottom rows to the sides of the middle row. The Wrench block is now complete.

7. Repeat steps 3 through 6 until all the blocks needed are assembled. Finish the project as described in the Introduction.

Note: An optional addition gives this pattern a slightly different look. This is achieved by adding triangles to the edges of the block. A larger block, of course, is created, and the resulting pattern can be rotated 45 degrees.

The quilts in the photograph on page 48 and in drawing 1 are reversals of each other. Here it is easy to see how transposing the light and dark elements creates a different visual effect. These two designs show a very basic rendering of the wrench. The colors in drawing 1 are characteristic of Amish quilts. In 2 the center square becomes part of the background, and the wrench is made more solid-looking by using the same color for all the narrow rectangular strips. Number 3 is similar, except that in this case the wrench is made of two colors. Number 4 uses black and two shades of gray against a white background to create a more sophisticated effect. In design 5 the eye is simultaneously drawn by the white triangles, the yellow background, and the strong lines of the gray. Number 6 uses a cross motif, and in 7 a bright red X, formed by four corner triangles and the center square, stands out against a white background. The center square in 8 is absorbed into the background and the four triangles dominate the design. Number 9 creates squares for a very graphic effect.

Pattern
Pieces

Shown full size

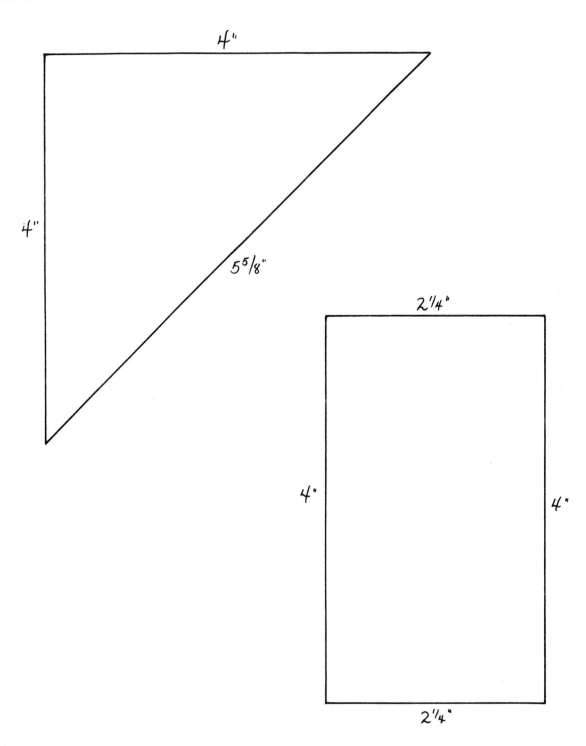

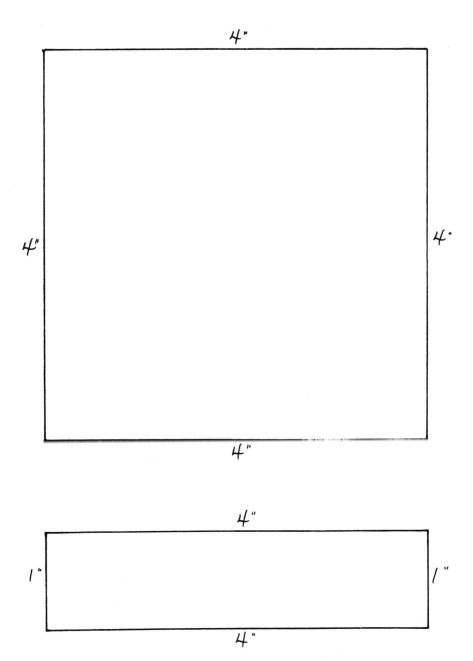

7.
Double Nine-Patch

Also known as Nine-Patch Cross, Double Nine-Patch is one of the easiest patterns to piece, yet one of the most versatile. Its basic unit is a square composed of nine smaller squares. Nine of these nine-patch squares are joined to form a larger block. Usually, four of the nine-patch squares are of the same color. If this traditional arrangement is followed, it is easier to use one piece for the solid squares instead of nine. For this purpose, a large square pattern is included in the instructions along with the standard square.

Piecing Instructions

1. Measure the bed for which the quilt is intended, as described in the Introduction. Decide whether or not sashes will be used between the Double Nine-Patch blocks and how wide they will be. Using sashes of some kind is advisable with this pattern. Next, calculate how many blocks will be needed. Each block is 18″ (45.7 cm) square, so with sashes of moderate width at least four blocks will be required for a crib quilt, twelve blocks for a twin-size bed, and sixteen blocks for a full, queen, or king-size bed. If especially wide or narrow sashes are used, no sashes at all, or if the bed is an unusual size, the number of blocks will of course vary. It may be necessary to adjust the size of the quilt so that the sashes running around the edges of the quilt can be of the same width since the numbers don't always come out quite right, and too much horizontal or vertical space is left over. In any case, each 18″ (45.7 cm) Double Nine-Patch block will require ¾ yards (68.6 cm) of fabric.

2. Cut all of the pattern pieces, lining up the arrows on the pattern with the straight grain of the fabric and leaving seam allowances of at least ¼″ (6 mm).

3. Select one of the nine nine-patch blocks and sew its top row by joining three squares of the appropriate color(s). Open and press seams.

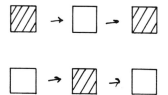

4. Sew the middle row and the bottom row in the same fashion. Open and press seams.

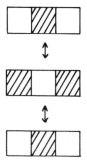

5. Attach the top to the middle row, then these two rows to the bottom row. Open and press seams.

6. Repeat steps 3 through 5 for the other eight nine-patch blocks.

7. Join the top three nine-patch blocks to form the top row of the Double Nine-Patch square. Open and press seams.

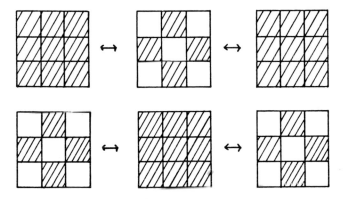

8. Sew the three middle blocks together and the three bottom blocks together. Open and press seams.

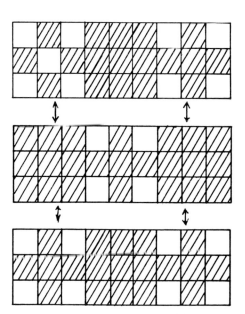

9. Attach the top row to one side of the middle row and the bottom row to the other side of the middle row. Open and press seams. You now have a completed Double Nine-Patch block. Attach blocks to sashes or to each other and finish the quilt as outlined in the Introduction.

Note: For an interesting variation, tilt the design by attaching triangular pieces to the sides of the block. This creates a larger square, with the Double Nine-Patch forming a diamond at its center.

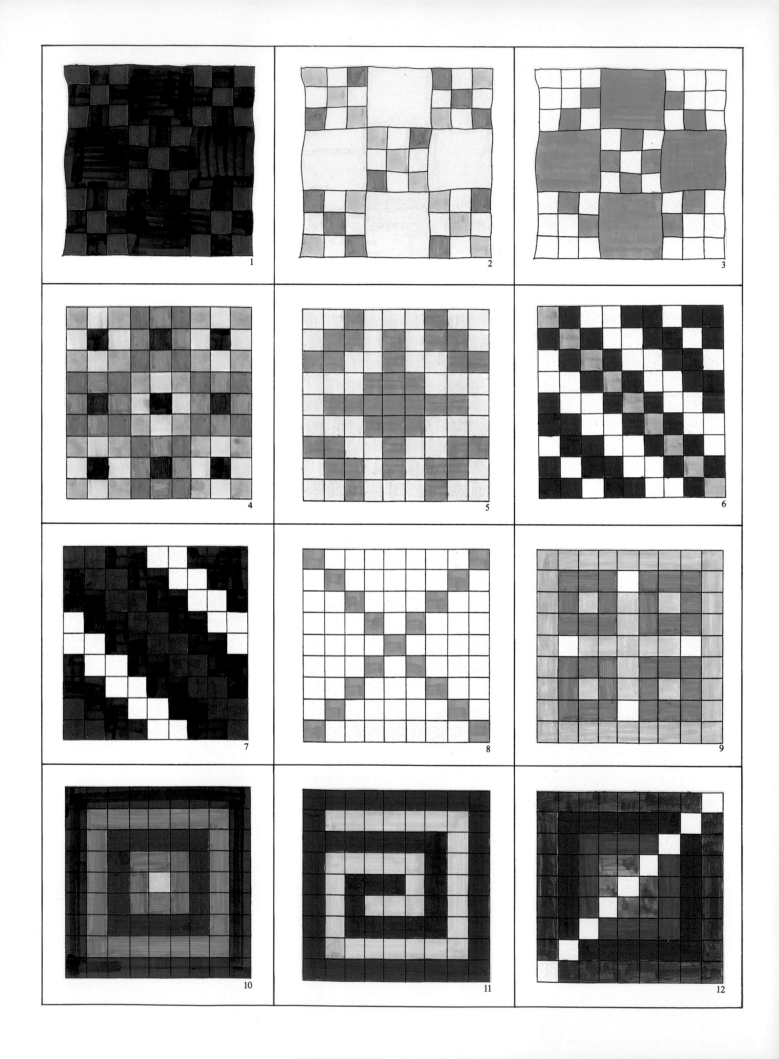

Pattern Pieces

Shown full size

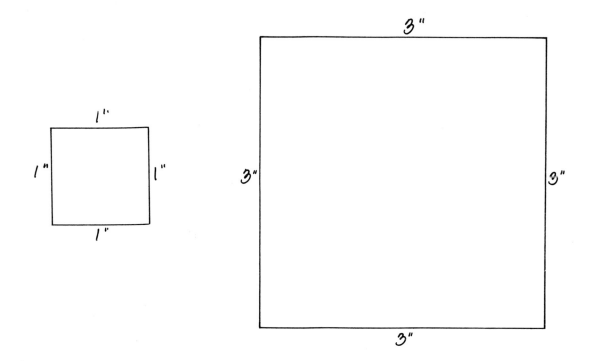

The quilts in the photograph on page 54 and in drawings 1 and 2 are all classic examples of this time-honored pattern. Number 1 is especially typical of the colors used in Amish quilts. Number 2 is perfect for a child's room or a crib quilt since it incorporates both pink and blue. Drawing 3 continues to use four large single-colored squares as part of the design, but in a less traditional fashion. The other things that can be done with Double Nine-Patch are shown in 4 through 8. In number 4 gray and blue boxes with dark centers draw the eye first to one, then another, part of the block. Number 5 has a cross as the dominant feature. Numbers 6 and 7 concentrate on diagonal lines—6 has a soft, pastel look, and 7 is a powerful, jagged approach. Number 8, when used without sashes, becomes a variation of another popular pattern, Single Irish Chain (not to be confused with Irish Chain, see chapter 15). Numbers 9 and 10 emphasize large squares in a modernistic approach. In 9 the four dark-blue squares compete with the single light-blue square for the eye's attention; in 10 a black border creates a frame from which a tunnel recedes. Bright colors assist in this illusion of depth. Number 11 is a variation of the classical Greek Key pattern, and in 12 white squares against a background of bright colors create a diagonal row of steps.

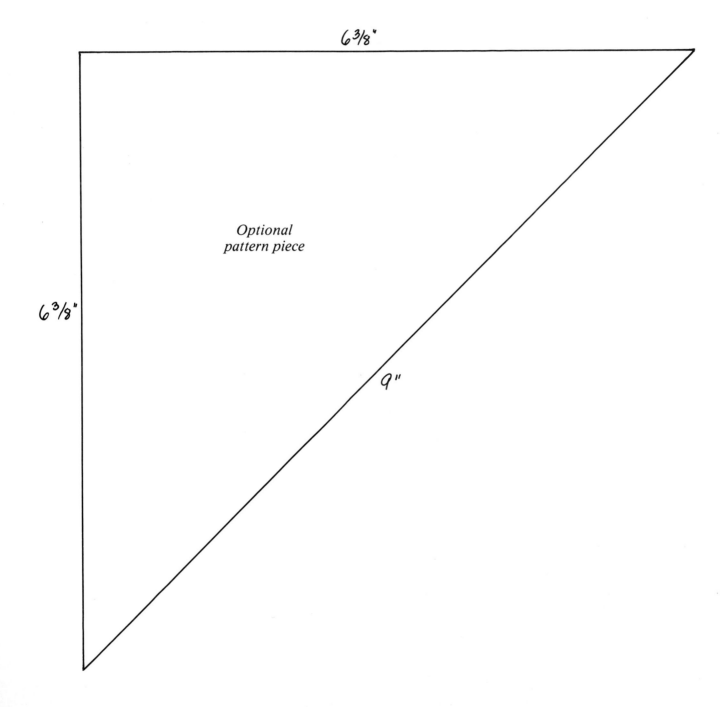

8.
Rabbit's Paw

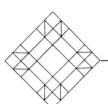

Although a rabbit's paw is probably not readily visible at first viewing, this pattern is an intriguing one all the same. Found primarily in Amish quilts, it is less well known than many of the other patterns included in this book. A total of thirty-seven pieces are needed to create each block.

Piecing Instructions

1. Measure the bed for which the quilt is intended, as described in the Introduction. Decide whether sashes will be used between the Rabbit's Paw blocks and how wide they will be. Next, calculate how many blocks are needed. Each block is 12″ (30.5 cm) square, so with sashes of moderate width at least four blocks are required for a crib quilt, twenty-four for a twin-size bed, and thirty for a full, queen, or king-size bed. If especially wide or narrow sashes are used, no sashes at all, or if the bed is an unusual size, the number of blocks will of course vary. It may also be necessary to adjust the size of the quilt slightly so that the sashes running around the edges of the quilt can be the same width since the numbers don't always come out quite right and too much vertical or horizontal space is left over. Each block requires at least ⅓ to ½ yard (30.5 cm to 45.7 cm) of fabric and calls for four large triangles, sixteen small triangles, one large square, eight small squares, and eight rectangles.

2. Cut all the pattern pieces, lining up the arrows on the pattern with the straight grain of the fabric and leaving seam allowances of at least ¼″ (6 mm).

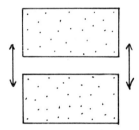

3. Think of the diamond-shaped main design of Rabbit's Paw as a square; if it helps, turn the page 45 degrees and take a good look at the square. It has three rows. The top row, from left to right, is composed of a square made of eight triangles and two squares; a square made of two horizontal rectangles; and another square made of eight triangles and two squares.

   The bottom row is exactly like the top row. The middle row is the simplest. From left to right, it has a square made of two vertical rectangles, a large plain square, and another square made of two vertical rectangles.

   Begin by sewing together pairs of rectangular pieces along their long sides so that they form squares. Open and press seams.

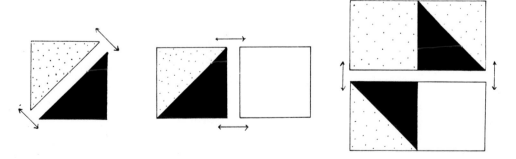

4. Next, construct the composite squares. These are a little more complicated. Join the small triangles into pairs so that they become small squares. Open and press seams. Now sew each pair of triangles to a plain square. (Make sure the correct pair of triangles is attached to the correct square!) Open and press seams. Join the resulting rectangles to each other so that they form 2¾″ (7 cm) squares; make certain, as you pin and sew, that each triangle-square is facing a plain square and vice versa.

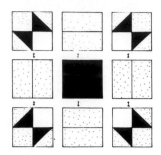

5. Now build the horizontal rows of the pattern. Attach a composite square to each side of a horizontal rectangular pair; this will be the top row. Attach a rectangular group to each side. Repeat; this will be the bottom row. Form the middle row by attaching a pair of vertical rectangles to each side of the plain 2¾″ (7 cm) square.

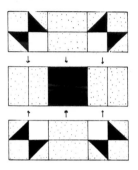

6. Sew the top and bottom rows to each side of the middle row. You should now have an 8½″ (21.6 cm) square. Open and press seams.

7. Sew one of the large triangles to each side of the square. The main design thus becomes a large diamond in the center of a plain square. The Rabbit's Paw block is now complete.

8. Repeat steps 3 through 7 until all the blocks needed are in hand. Finish the quilt as outlined in the Introduction.

All of these variations on Rabbit's Paw have a similar motif—a cross of sorts or a central diamond with points at each corner. In some cases, as in design 1 (opposite) and the quilt in the photograph on page 62, the cross is well-defined and rather traditional. In 2 the points are seen as V's and in 3 they appear as curls. Number 4 is an X. Numbers 5 through 9 illustrate how the addition or elimination of one diamond at each corner directs the eye toward or away from the central diamond.

Numbers 10 and 11 show how by coloring the four small corner diamonds distinctly from any other element in the block, the eye can be drawn to the edge of the square, and away from the central shape in the block. Number 12 creates a pattern of diamonds and rectangles for a classic patchwork effect.

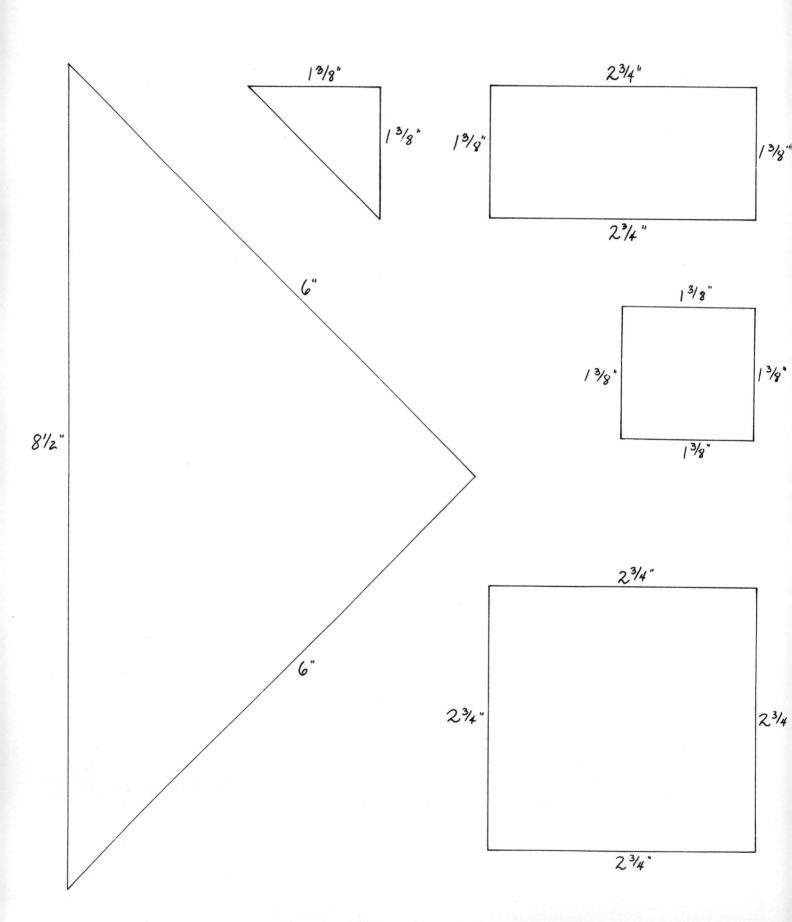

9. Bow-Tie

There are two ways of constructing a Bow-Tie square. Which one is chosen is entirely a matter of personal preference. One method creates the diamond-shaped centers of each bow-tie by joining four triangles, the other by appliquéing one square.

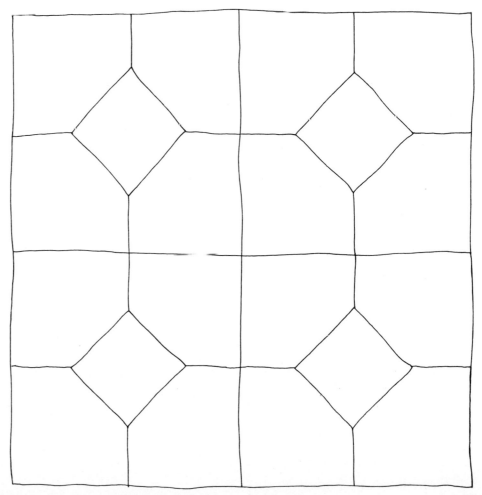

Piecing Instructions

Method 1

The advantage of this method is that appliqué work is not necessary, a process that terrifies most beginning quilters. The disadvantage is that for every block of four bow-ties, thirty-two pieces will have to be cut and pieced instead of twenty.

1. Measure the bed for which the quilt is intended, as described in the Introduction. Decide whether sashes will be used between the Bow-Tie blocks and how wide they will be; Bow-Tie lends itself equally well to quilts with and without sashes. Next, calculate how many blocks will be needed. Each block is 12″ (30.5 cm) square, so with sashes of moderate width at least four blocks are necessary for a crib quilt, twenty-four for a twin-size bed, and thirty for a full, queen, or king-size bed. If especially wide or narrow sashes are used, no sashes at all, or if the bed is an unusual size, the number of blocks will of course vary. It may also be necessary to adjust the size of the quilt slightly so that the sashes running around the edges of the quilt can be the same width; sometimes the numbers don't always come out quite right and too much vertical or horizontal space is left over. In any case, each 12″ (30.5 cm) Bow-Tie block will require ⅜ yards (34.3 cm) of fabric.

2. Cut all the pattern pieces, lining up the arrows on the pattern with the straight grain of the fabric and leaving seam allowances of at least ¼″ (6 mm).

3. Create four squares by sewing the triangles to the diagonal edges of the "squares" (the pattern piece that looks like a square with one corner missing). Remember that sewing is along the bias here and that as a result the material will be more likely to stretch and pucker. Open and press the seams.

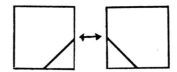

4. Sew the squares into two pairs of squares, with the triangular sections facing each other. Make sure if patterned fabrics are used that all the patterns are facing the way intended. Open and press seams.

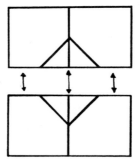

5. Sew the pairs of squares together. The two triangular sections will now form a diamond. Open and press seams.

6. Repeat steps 3 through 5 three more times. There will now be four squares, each with a diamond in its center.

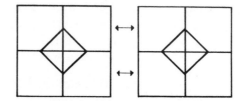

7. Sew these squares into two pairs. Open and press seams.

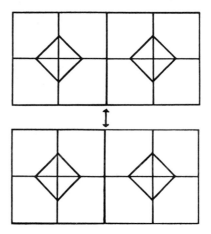

8. Sew the pairs together. Open and press seams. A Bow-Tie block is now complete.

Method 2

1. Follow steps 1 and 2 of Method 1.

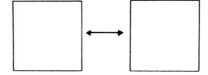

2. Sew two squares together to make a rectangle. Use the 3″ (7.6 cm) pattern pieces which do not appear to have a corner missing. Open and press seams. Repeat.

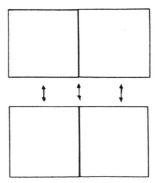

3. Sew the two rectangles together to make a square. Open and press seams.

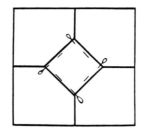

4. Center a 2″ (5.1 cm) square over the intersection of the four squares. Fold the seam allowances under and pin in place. Blindstitch it to the four squares and remove pins.

5. Repeat steps 2 through 4 three times. There will now be four squares, each with a diamond in its center.

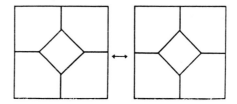

6. Sew these squares into two pairs. Open and press seams.

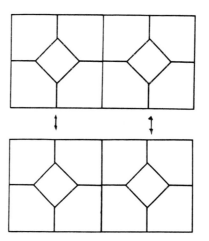

7. Sew the pairs together. Open and press seams. A Bow-Tie block is now complete.

8. Attach the blocks and finish the quilt as outlined in the Introduction.

Pattern Pieces

Shown full size

Method 2 pattern pieces

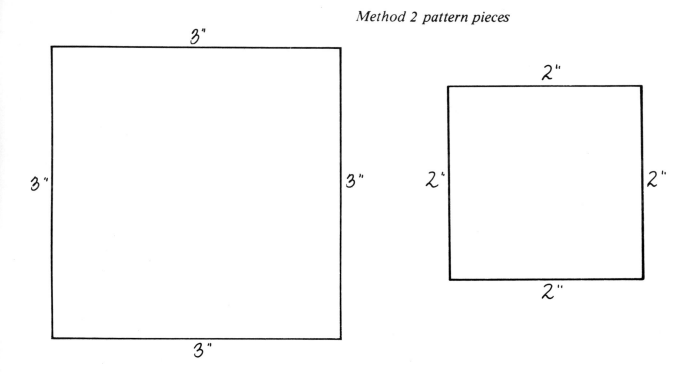

Method 1 pattern pieces

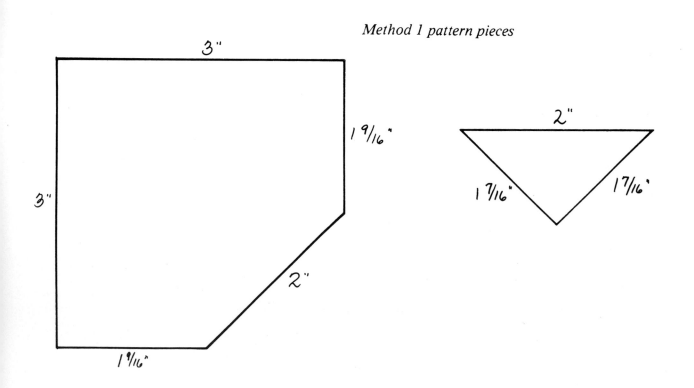

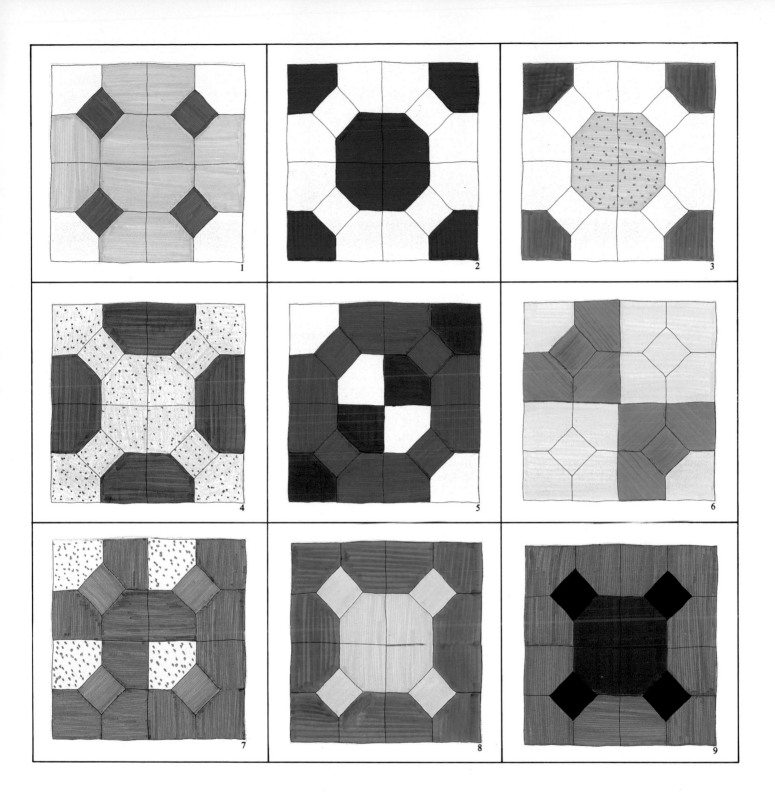

*The quilt in the photograph on page 68 is a perfect example of this design —
brightly colored "ties" all pointed the same way. But are the ties formed by the
lighter or darker color? Do they point to the left or the right? As in many pieced
designs a pattern can be viewed in several ways. In drawing 1 the ties disappear,
subsumed into a cross dotted with diamonds. Numbers 2 and 3 have the ties
facing toward each other, forming a ring. An X is created in 4 by light-colored
ties pointing outward against a dark background. Number 5 preserves the ring
seen in 2 and 3, but here the background is split into four quadrants. In 6, 7, 8,
and 9 the bow ties are hardly visible at all. Number 6 features two L-shaped
figures pointing in opposite directions, 7 has four of these figures, and in 8 a
dark border frames a light center. Number 9 reverses the design of 8.*

10.
Hexagon

This exceptionally versatile pattern has been used to produce a great number of remarkable quilts, including some with over 60,000 pieces. It is not really intended to be used in blocks with sashes dividing them; the full effect is best appreciated when the pattern dominates the entire quilt. The basic block requires forty-nine pieces.

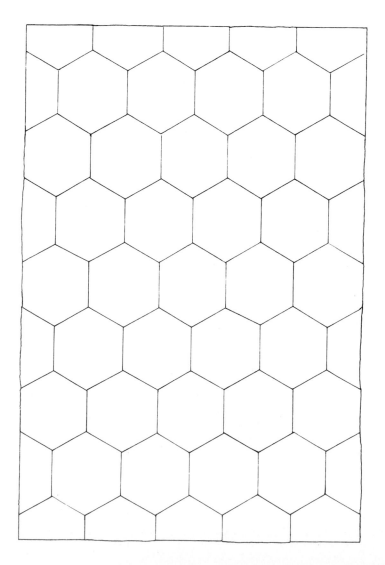

Piecing Instructions

1. Measure the bed for which the quilt is intended, as described in the Introduction. The rectangular area in the photograph measures 13″ wide by 19″ long (33 cm by 48.3 cm); it is composed of thirty-nine whole hexagons, ten hexagons divided horizontally, and eight hexagons divided vertically. This 13″ by 19″ block can be added to others. It is designed so that the edges will meet. All that is needed is a little math.

   If, for example, the finished quilt is to measure 78″ by 99″ (198 cm by 252 cm), five blocks, each 13″ (33 cm) wide, will be needed to cover that width. At least five blocks, each 19″ (48.3 cm) long, will be needed to cover the length. Five times nineteen is 95, so 4″ (10.2 cm) of space is left over. There are three options: make the quilt a little shorter than planned; make it a little longer and cut it off at the nearest convenient point (in this case, 5½″ [14 cm] will include first a row of full hexagons, another row of full hexagons, and a bottom row of half-hexagons); or figure out how much of the pattern must be repeated to provide exactly 4″ (10.2 cm) more of length, and adapt the templates to suit the purpose. The first and second options, obviously, are somewhat easier than the third. In our example, if the second option were chosen, enough fabric would have to be bought for twenty-five full blocks of the hexagon pattern, plus five 13″ by 5½″ (33 cm by 14 cm) blocks.

   Remember that when joining the blocks, some of the half-hexagons will become complete hexagons. If math is not your strong point, each block can be simply pieced on its own, joining them all together at the end to form the quilt top. The problem with this is that the seams running through the middle of some of the hexagons will look a little obvious. My advice is to take the time to sit down and figure out exactly how many half-hexagons will be completed—and, therefore, how many half- and complete hexagons are needed to mark and cut. The energy expended at the outset in planning and calculation won't be wasted. If the hexagons are made continuous, fewer scraps of cloth will have to be cut and pieced, and the end result will be more attractive.

   Each 13″ by 19″ (33 cm by 48.3 cm) block of the Hexagon pattern requires ⅓ to ½ yard (30.5 cm to 45.7 cm) of fabric.

2. Cut all the pattern pieces, lining up the arrows on the pattern with the straight grain of the fabric and leaving seam allowances of at least ¼″ (6 mm).

Easily one of the most versatile quilt patterns, Hexagon can be rendered as a collection of small rings as in the photograph on the next page; a group of larger concentric shapes as in 1 and 2 (see page 77); a series of vertical rows, 3; diagonal rows, 4, 5, and 6; a flamestitch or chevron design, 7; irregular diagonal rows, 8; or a multicolor honeycomb, 9. On a larger scale than is shown here, and especially if smaller hexagons are used, extraordinarily elaborate designs can be created, including interlocking bands of color and large multicolor stars.

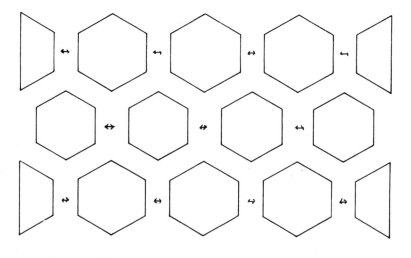

3. Sew the hexagons together in horizontal rows, opening and pressing seams

as you go along. Do not sew into the seam allowances here, or it will be impossible to join the rows.

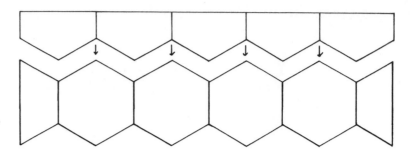

4. Sew the horizontal rows together to form the quilt top. The pinning and sewing of these rows may seem difficult at first but then becomes easier. Open and press seams.

Pattern Pieces

Shown full size

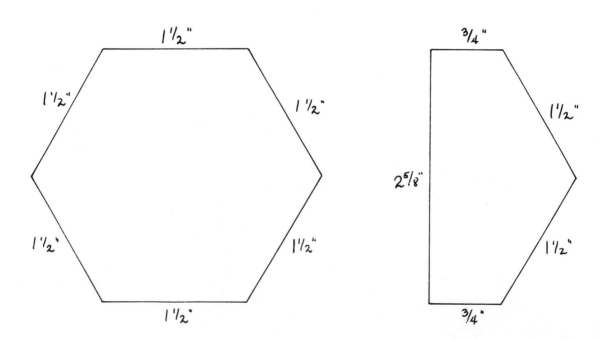

11.
Pineapple Log Cabin

Pineapple Log Cabin is the exotic cousin of the ordinary Log Cabin—and it's almost as easy, I promise. The thing that frightens some beginning quilters is the idea of dealing with trapezoids instead of safe, comfortable, familiar rectangles. Only thirty-seven pieces are needed to complete a Pineapple Log Cabin block, and they are not difficult to produce.

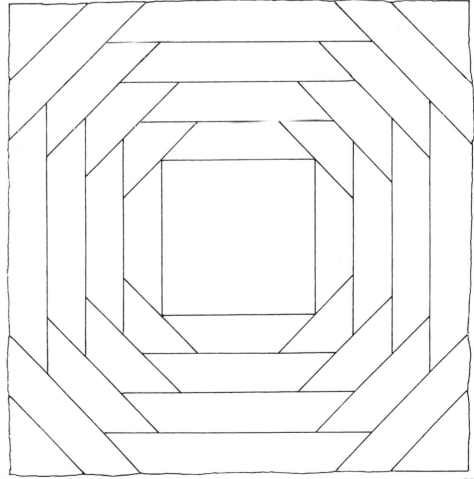

Piecing Instructions

1. Measure the bed for which the quilt is intended, as described in the Introduction. This pattern is not really designed for use with sashes. Calculate how many blocks will be needed. Each block is 12″ (30.5 cm) square, so at least four blocks are required for a crib quilt, twenty-four for a twin-size bed, and thirty for a full, queen, or king-size bed. If the bed is an unusual size, the number of blocks will of course vary. Each 12″ (30.5 cm) block requires ⅔ yard (61 cm) of fabric and has thirty-seven pieces: one 4″ (10.2 cm) square, four triangles—the base of each being 3″ (7.6 cm)—and thirty-two trapezoids, the measure of each being the longest side: four, 2¾″ (7 cm); four, 3½″ (8.9 cm); four, 4″ (10.2 cm); four, 4¼″ (10.8 cm); eight, 5″ (12.7 cm); four, 6″ (15.2 cm); and four, 7″ (17.8 cm).

2. Cut all the pattern pieces, lining up the arrows on the pattern with the straight grain of the fabric and leaving seam allowances of at least ¼″ (6 mm).

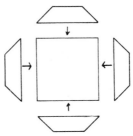

3. Take the four trapezoids whose longest sides are 4″ (10.2 cm) and attach them to the four sides of the 4″ (10.2 cm) square, long sides touching the square, short sides facing outward. Open and press seams.

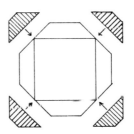

4. Attach the four trapezoids whose longest sides are 2¾″ (7 cm) to the corners, so that the final shape looks like a 6″ (15.2 cm) square with just the tips sliced off.

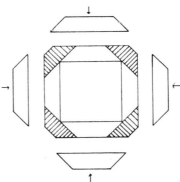

5. Sew four of the trapezoids whose longest sides are 5″ (12.7 cm) to the sides of the "square," so that an octagon is formed. Open and press seams.

6. Attach the four trapezoids whose longest sides are 3½″ (8.9 cm) to the corners, making the shape look like an 8″ square (20.3 cm) with the tips cut off.

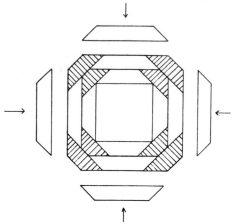

7. Sew the four trapezoids whose longest sides are 6″ (15.2 cm) to the sides of the "square" so that it looks like a stop sign again. Open and press seams.

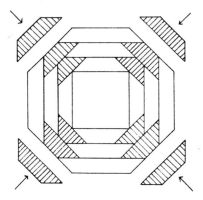

8. Attach the four trapezoids whose longest sides are 4¼″ (10.8 cm) to the corners, producing the "square" shape again, this time a 10″ (25.4 cm) "square."

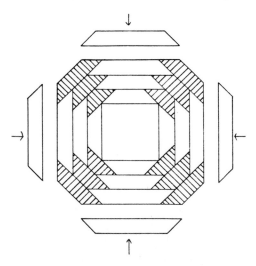

9. Sew the four trapezoids whose longest sides are 7″ (17.8 cm) to the sides of the "square," producing the octagonal shape. Open and press seams.

Drawing 1 above and the quilt in the photograph on page 80 are simple, straight-forward versions of this basic design, varying only in the color and size of the central block. Design 2 adds two vertical colored strips. Numbers 3, 4, and 5 emphasize the squares in the design. Number 6 creates a spiral pattern. Number 7 uses multicolored strips randomly placed. The corners of the block are emphasized in 8, and 9 softens the vertical stripes to create a pineapple effect.

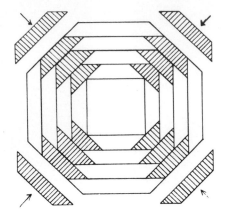

10. Attach the four remaining trapezoids whose longest sides are 5″ (12.7 cm) to the corners. Open and press seams.

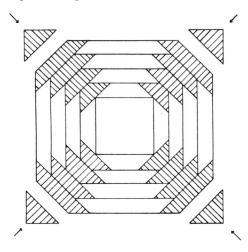

11. Attach the triangles to the corners, completing the square.

12. Repeat steps 3 through 11 until all the blocks are assembled. Finish the quilt as outlined in the Introduction.

Pattern Pieces

Shown full size

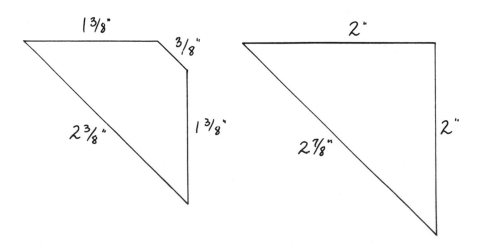

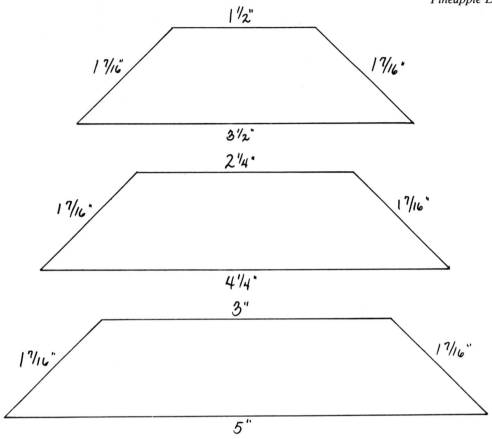

1½"

1 7/16"   1 7/16"

3½"

2¼"

1 7/16"   1 7/16"

4¼"

3"

1 7/16"   1 7/16"

5"

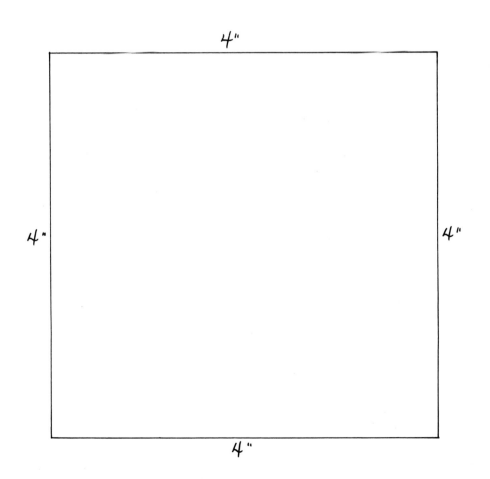

4"

4"   4"

4"

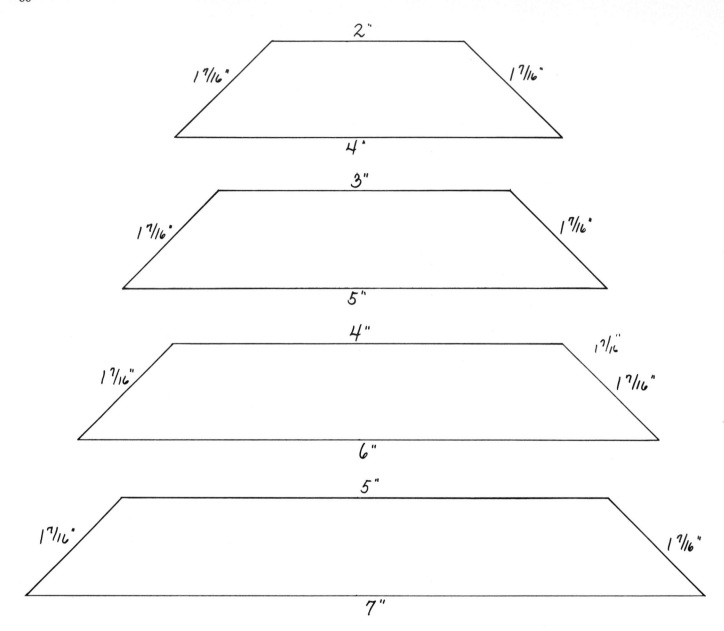

12.
Log Cabin

This pattern requires the cutting and piecing of more different sized scraps of cloth than almost any other in this book, but it's worth it. Few designs are more resonant of American history, and few, I think, are more beautiful. But, then, perhaps I'm biased; my first quilt was a Log Cabin. The basic 12" (30.5 cm) block contains twenty-one pieces and is manageable by any patient quilter.

Piecing Instructions

1. Measure the bed for which the quilt is intended, as described in the Introduction. Log Cabin is not intended for use with sashes, but there is some leeway if the length or width of the quilt is not meant to be a multiple of 12″ (30.5 cm) (the size of the Log Cabin block). Log Cabin is constructed by adding a series of border strips to a central square, and each ring of border strips adds 2″ (5.1 cm) to the overall dimensions of the block. So, if you simply don't add the last set of border strips, you have a 10″ (25.4 cm) block. If you don't add the next-to-last set as well, you have an 8″ (20.3 cm) block. The 12″ (30.5 cm) block requires 3½ yards (3.20 m) of fabric and has twenty-one individual pieces: one 2″ (5.1 cm) square piece and twenty 1″ (2.5 cm) wide strips of various lengths—one 2″ (5.1 cm), two 3″ (7.6 cm), two 4″ (10.2 cm), two 5″ (12.7 cm), two 6″ (15.2 cm), two 7″ (17.8 cm), two 8″ (20.3 cm), two 9″ (22.9 cm), two 10″ (25.4 cm), two 11″ (27.8 cm), and one 12″ (30.5 cm). The photograph shows a set of twelve 12″ (30.5 cm) blocks.

2. Cut all the pattern pieces, lining up the arrows on the pattern with the straight grain of the fabric and leaving seam allowances of at least ¼″ (6 mm).

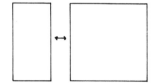

3. Sew the 1″ by 2″ (2.5 cm by 5.1 cm) strip to one side of the 2″ (5.1 cm) square piece. Open and press seams. Decide now whether this strip will end up on the right, the left, the top, or the bottom of the block. When beginning a new row of border strips, always start on the same side, and all of the finished blocks should be aligned the same way.

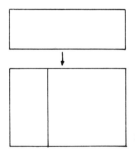

4. Sew one of the 1″ by 3″ (2.5 cm by 7.6 cm) strips along the edge of the attached square and 2″ strip (5.1 cm) so that it touches both of them and forms a square. Open and press seams.

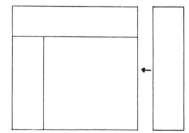

5. Sew the other 3″ (7.6 cm) strip so that it touches the 2″ (5.1 cm) square and the end of the first 3″ (7.6 cm) strip, forming a rectangle. Open and press seams.

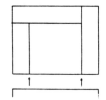

6. Sew one of the 4″ (10.2 cm) strips so that it touches the second 3″ (7.6 cm) strip, the 2″ (5.1 cm) square, and the 2″ (5.1 cm) strip, forming a square. This square should measure 4″ (10.2 cm) on each side.

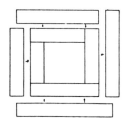

7. Repeat steps 3 through 6 with larger strips, starting on the side with the 2″ (5.1 cm) strip: add a 4″ (10.2 cm) strip, then a 5″ (12.7 cm) strip, then the second 5″ (12.7 cm) strip, and then a 6″ (15.2 cm) strip to form a square. Open and press seams.

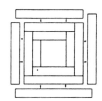

8. Repeat the procedure with even larger strips, again starting on the same side as before. Sew on the second 6″ (15.2 cm) strip, then a 7″ (17.8 cm) strip, the second 7″ (17.8 cm) strip, and finally an 8″ (20.3 cm) strip. Open and press seams. An 8″ (20.3 cm) square is now complete, and if the length and width of the finished quilt are to be multiples of 8″ (20.3 cm), stop here and repeat steps 3 through 8 until as many Log Cabin blocks as needed are completed. Finish the quilt as directed in the Introduction.

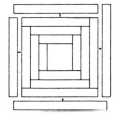

Log Cabin was an extremely popular pattern in the nineteenth century, and it has a number of traditional variations. The quilts in the photograph (next page) and in drawing 1 (page 91) are both examples of the Barn Raising variation, in which diamonds radiate from the center outward. Often, as is the case with these two examples, the pattern is achieved by using bright and pale versions of the same color scheme. However, Barn Raising can also combine fabrics of two distinct colors. Drawings 2 and 3 show another Log Cabin variation — Light and Dark. Large diamonds stand out in relief against each other, punctuated by the small squares along their sides. Number 2 is a more traditional rendering, while number 3 is a bolder, more modern arrangement. Drawing 4 is of still another popular rendition of Log Cabin, the Straight Furrow design. In 4 the colors follow an organized sequence, and contribute to an illusion of depth. These traditional variations are only a few of the ways in which Log Cabin can be used. Designs 5 through 9 show a variety of patterns that can be created by concentrating on the strip elements. Hourglasses are created in 5; pyramids with diagonal background rows are the subject of 6. Number 7 features zigzag rows with multicolored backgrounds; a Japanese lantern effect is created in 8; and huge V's are dominant in 9.

9. If blocks larger than 8″ (20.3 cm) are wanted, continue to add strips, starting always on the same side. Add an 8″ (20.3 cm) strip, then a 9″ (22.9 cm), the other 9″ (22.9 cm), and finally a 10″ (25.4 cm) strip. Open and press seams. One 10″ (25.4 cm) square is now completed, and if the length and width of the quilt are to be multiples of 10″ (25.4 cm), stop here and repeat steps 3 through 9 until as many Log Cabin blocks as needed are complete. Finish the quilt as directed in the Introduction.

10. If 12″ (30.5 cm) blocks are the aim, add the last round of border strips — a 10″ (25.4 cm), an 11″ (27.8 cm), another 11″ (27.8 cm) and the one 12″ (30.5 cm). One 12″ (30.5 cm) square has now been assembled. Repeat steps 3 through 10 until all the necessary blocks are finished. Assemble the quilt as directed in the Introduction.

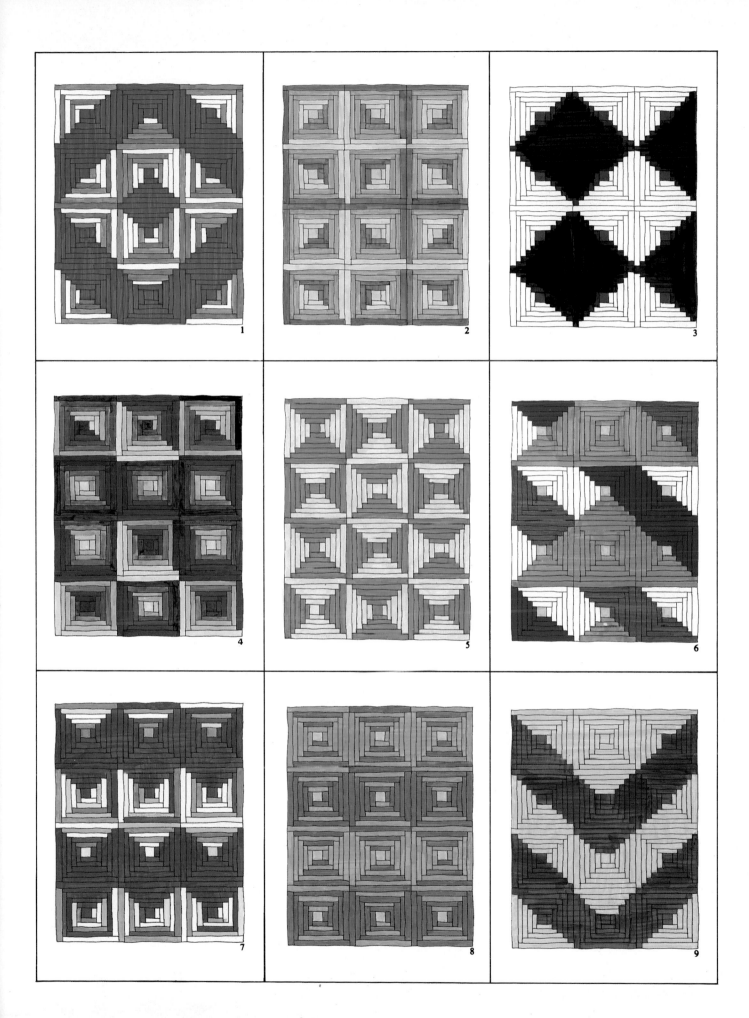

Pattern
Pieces

Shown one-half actual size

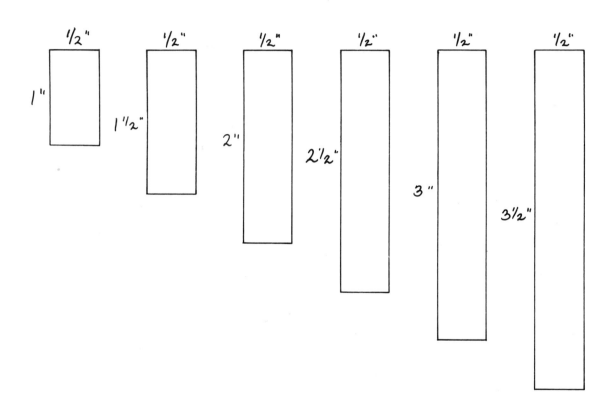

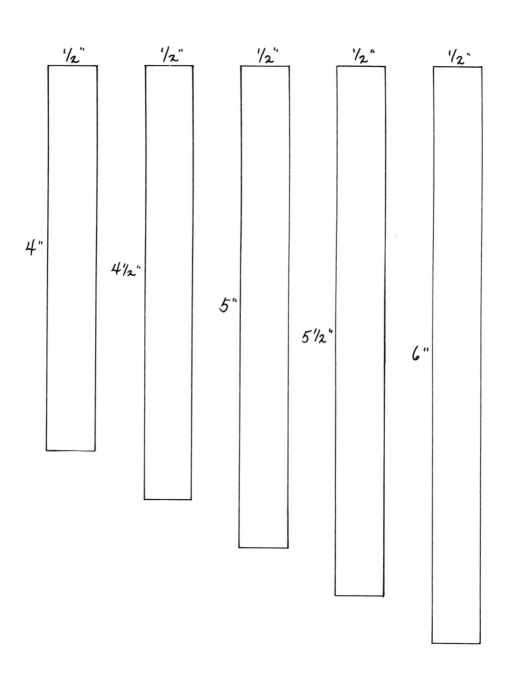

13.
Lone Star

Also called the Star of Bethlehem, Lone Star looks much more difficult than it actually is. A quilt might consist of only one star, a true lone star, made with diamonds that are 2" (5.1 cm) on each side, the overall pattern measuring 54" (137.2 cm). A quilt made up of a series of at least six stars is another alternative. The block would be half the size of the single star quilt or 27" (68.6 cm). It consists of 1" (2.5 cm) diamonds. Pattern pieces for both the 1" (2.5 cm) and 2" (5.1 cm) diamonds are provided. Both the 27" (68.6 cm) and the 54" (137.2 cm) blocks require 512 individual diamonds.

Piecing Instructions

1. Measure the bed for which the quilt is intended, as described in the Introduction. If the 54″ (137.2 cm) star is chosen, make the quilt top in exactly the same way as the quilt back. Buy extra-wide material or sew together two or three lengths of fabric. If sewing fabric together is necessary to make the top or the back, remember when calculating fabric needs to take seam allowances into account. When the plain quilt top and the 54″ (137.2 cm) star pieces are ready, the star pattern will be appliquéd to the top. Each 54″ (137.2 cm) star requires 2⅔ yards (2.43 m) of fabric.

   If, however, the choice is to make a series of smaller 27″ (68.6 cm) stars, it is easier to cut a 27″ (68.6 cm) square for each block and appliqué the stars individually. Decide how wide the sashes will be, and figure out how many blocks are needed. The large size of the block limits flexibility somewhat. A crib quilt is too small for a series of stars; twin and full beds should have about six stars; queen and king-size beds have room for about nine stars. It may be necessary to adjust the size of the quilt somewhat so that the sashes around the edges can be the same width. Sometimes the numbers don't come out quite right, and too much horizontal or vertical space is left over. Each 27″ (68.6 cm) star requires 1⅓ yards (1.22 m) of fabric.

2. Cut all the pattern pieces, lining up the arrows on the pattern with the straight grain of the fabric and leaving seam allowances of at least ¼″ (6 mm).

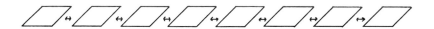

3. Pick one of the eight large diamond-shaped sections that make up the star and decide which row of small diamonds will be the "top" row. I find that the best way to avoid confusion with so many little diamonds running around is to make a drawing and mark it with the colors being used. That way it can be followed and the diamonds are not sewn together in the wrong order. The basic pattern grid shown in this chapter will be useful for this purpose.

   Piece together the eight diamonds in the "top" or first row, pressing seams open. The easiest mistake to make at this point is in the pinning of the diamonds before sewing begins; make sure the points line up correctly

---

Perhaps more than any other popular pattern, Lone Star lends itself to the use of bright, vibrant colors. Typically the colors radiate from the center outward in a magnificent sunburst, as in drawing 1 (opposite). But the quilt in the photograph on page 94 shows how the positioning of white with red, medium gray, and a black calico gives a crisp look, retains the sunburst, and makes the star appear to spin. In drawings 2 and 3 the stars are less like sunbursts than giant snowflakes. Lone Star also lends itself well to the use of pastels, as in 4, and if a lighter shade is used for the points, the sharp angles of the pattern are softened and appear rounded. Number 5 shows how Lone Star can be made to resemble a stained-glass flower, and 6 gives the illusion of a series of rooftops.

or lopsided diamonds will result. When all eight diamonds have been pieced together, they should look like a nice straight row of squares that just got squashed down to one side.

4. Repeat this procedure for the other seven rows, being careful to line up the diamonds correctly and to get the colors in the right order.

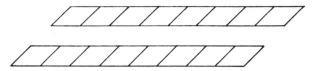

5. Attach the first to the second row, the third to the fourth, the fifth to the six, and the seventh to the eighth. Open and press seams.

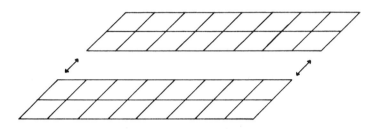

6. Attach the first and second rows to the third and fourth. Open and press seams. Attach the fifth and sixth rows to the seventh and eighth. Open and press seams.

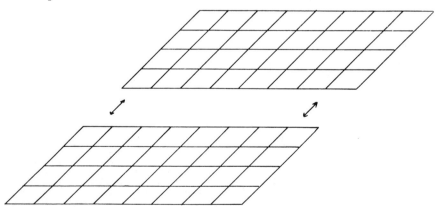

7. Attach rows one through four to five through eight. Open and press seams.

8. Repeat steps 3 through 7 seven times.

9. Sew the large diamond-shaped sections together in pairs. Do not sew into the seam allowances! You will not be able to appliqué the star to the backing if you do. Open and press seams. Sew the pairs together so that they make groups of four. Open and press seams. Sew the groups of four together to make the complete star. Open and press seams.

If a 54″ (137.2 cm) star is being made, center it on the quilt top and pin and baste in place. Blindstitch around the edges; remove the pins but not the basting. Remove basting stitches only after quilting is complete.

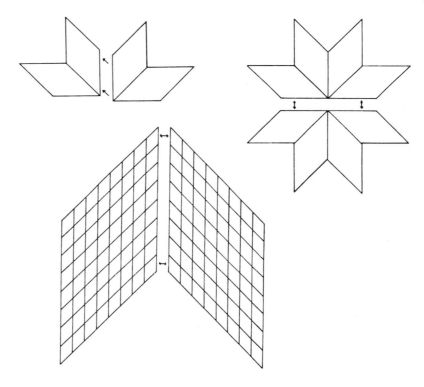

If 27" (68.6 cm) stars are being made, center each star on a 27" (68.6 cm) background block and pin and baste in place, leaving the knots on the top face of the square, not the back. Blindstitch around the edges and remove the pins but not the basting. Remove the basting stitches only when the project has been fully assembled and quilted.

10. Finish the quilt as described in the Introduction.

Pattern Pieces

Shown full size

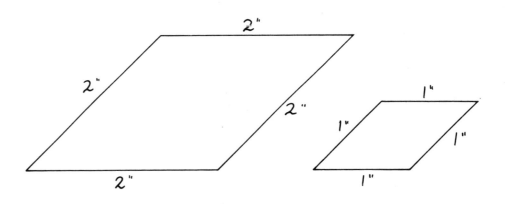

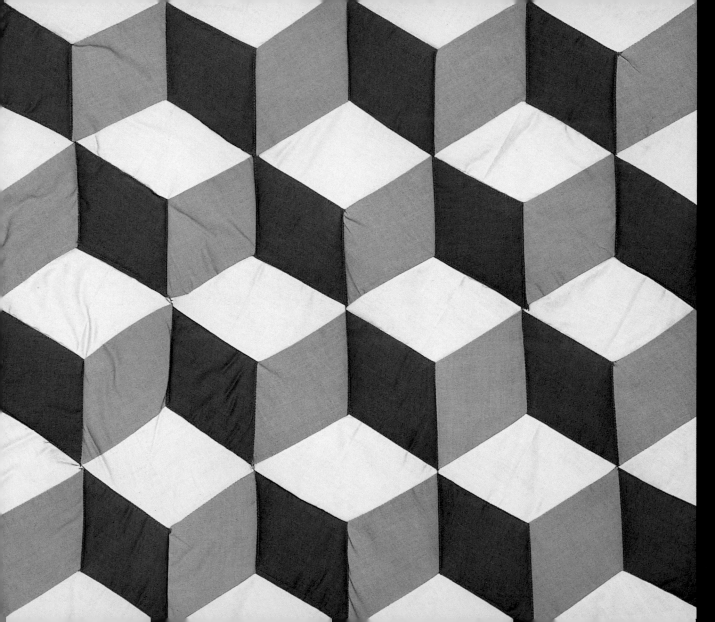

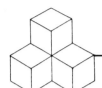

14.
Tumbling Blocks

Few patterns have the depth and the potential complexity of Tumbling Blocks. Judicious use of color can result in the blocks tumbling up or down, or to the side. Or, if you like, the blocks can fade away entirely, replaced by six-pointed stars. Whatever the choice, fifty-four pieces— all diamond forms—are needed for each quilt block.

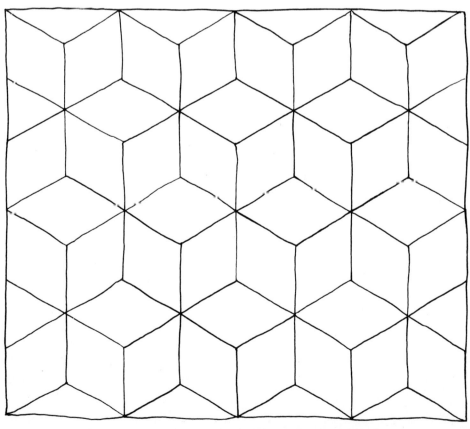

Piecing Instructions

1. Measure the bed for which the quilt is intended, as described in the Introduction. Since Tumbling Blocks is an overall design, not one that separates easily into blocks, it requires a little extra thought and attention at the outset. The area shown in the photograph measures 20″ (50.8 cm) wide by 18″ (45.7 cm) long and has forty-two complete diamonds, four diamonds split in half vertically, and eight diamonds split in half horizontally. This area is designed so that other areas of the same size may be joined to it without interruption in the pattern. The number of these "blocks" that will fit in the space allotted now has to be figured.

   For example, let's say a 108″ (274.2 cm) square quilt is the final size desired. Six of these blocks would fit perfectly to fill the vertical space—6 x 18″ = 108″ (6 x 45.7 cm = 274.2 cm). However, the horizontal space is a little trickier, since the block is not perfectly square. Five blocks across would fill 100″ (254 cm)—5 x 20″ = 100″ or 5 x 50.8 cm = 254 cm—so there are 8″ (20.2 cm) left to fill. The most accurate, but most difficult, approach is to calculate how much of the pattern is contained in 8″ (20.2 cm). Another approach is to fudge a little and get an easier number to work with—in this case, 10″ (25.4 cm). By adding 2″ (5.1 cm) to the width of the quilt, the area in the photograph is simply cut in half, right down the middle. The finished quilt would be 110″ (279.4 cm) wide and 108″ (274.2 cm) long: five-and-a-half blocks by six blocks.

   One more note: as long as all this math has to be done to figure out how many blocks are needed, determine how many of those half-diamonds will be completed when other blocks are added. If the thought of even more math is a deterrent, each area can be made separately, joining them all together to make the quilt top. In that case, seams will run through the middle of some of the diamonds. Especially if the number of blocks needed don't come out perfectly, those seams are going to look a little funny. It is worth doing the extra arithmetic.

   Each 20″ by 18″ (50.8 cm by 45.7 cm) area requires ¾ yard (0.69 m) of fabric.

2. Cut all the pattern pieces, lining up the arrows on the pattern with the straight grain of the fabric and leaving seam allowances of at least ¼″ (6 mm).

3. It helps when piecing Tumbling Blocks to think of it as horizontal rows of hexagons. Begin at the left-hand side of the top row. All of the hexagons in the top row will look as if someone clipped off the very top edge, but ignore this effect.

   (a) Attach the bottom two-thirds of the hexagons along a straight edge so that they look like an open book. Open and press seams.

   (b) Then cap those two pieces with one of the diamonds split in half horizontally. Repeat until enough hexagons are finished for the top row. The technique of capping the "open books" will seem strange at first; it takes some getting used to.

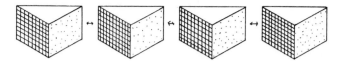

4. Attach the hexagons so that the half-diamonds all face upward, forming a straight edge. Open and press seams.

5. (a). Make the hexagons for the other rows in the same way, only with whole diamonds capping the "open books" instead of half-diamonds. (In other words, these will be real hexagons, not slightly truncated ones.) Sew into rows as was done with the top row. Open and press seams.

(b) Some hexagons run off the edges of the quilt and are therefore divided in half vertically. Make these by sewing a whole diamond to a diamond split in half vertically, and add them to the ends of alternate rows. This keeps the edge of the quilt straight along the sides.

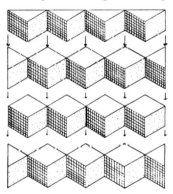

6. Sew the horizontal rows together to make the quilt top. Like making the hexagons, joining the rows together will seem strange at first because the line being sewn zigzags instead of being perfectly straight.

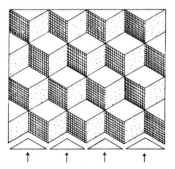

7. After all of the rows of hexagons have been sewn together, a zigzaggy edge will be left at the very bottom. Straighten this out by using diamonds split horizontally to complete the design.

8. Finish the quilt as described in the Introduction.

Pattern Pieces

Shown full size

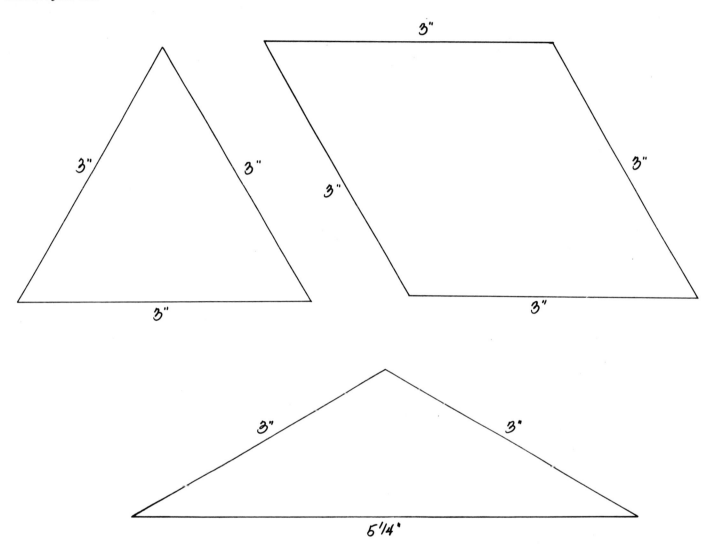

The quilt in the photograph (page 100) is a classic example of this popular pattern. Depending on the use of color and on one's perspective, the blocks appear to "tumble" to the left, the right, up, or down. In drawing 1, the gradations of color and the use of black for two sides of each block make the pattern less ambiguous. This color combination is based on that of an Amish quilt. Number 2 can be perceived as a series of blocks pointing to the left or right, or as a series of ribbons or diagonal rows. Number 3 forms a series of steps, and 4 creates multicolored three-dimensional cubes. Numbers 5 through 9 abandon the block theory entirely, using the same diamond-shaped pieces to create six-pointed stars as in 5 or a studded ring as in 6. In 7 three-dimensional blocks encircle a floral motif, and in 8 two interpretations emerge: a series of solid flowers over a multicolored background, or chains of three-dimensional blocks over a solid ground. In 9 solid flowers or stars are set against a multicolored background.

15.
Irish Chain

Irish Chain is a wonderfully versatile pattern. However, like some other patterns included in this book, it doesn't break down into blocks very well. That means a little more planning is required to estimate fabric needs and to make the project proceed smoothly.

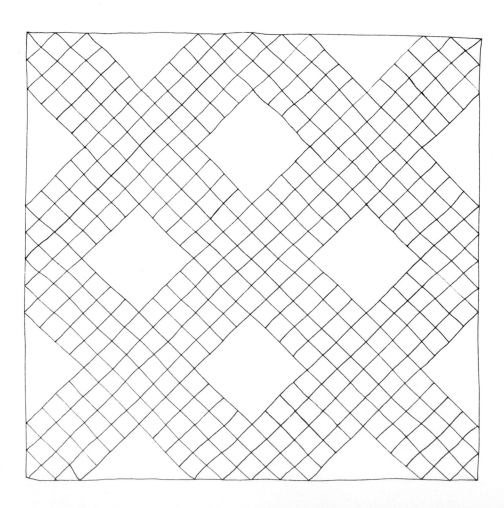

Piecing Instructions

1. Measure the bed for which the quilt is intended, as described in the Introduction. Since Irish Chain is not designed for use in blocks separated by sashes, a slightly different procedure to estimate fabric requirements must be followed.

   The area shown in the photograph measures 46″ (116.8 cm) square. It is composed of 4 large blocks, 8 halves of large blocks, 368 small blocks, and 32 halves of small blocks. It requires 3 yards (2.74 m) of fabric.

   All or part of other 46″ (116.8 cm) areas may be attached to this one; it is designed so that it will line up correctly. Unless a 92″ square (233.7 cm) quilt is wanted, I suggest that the design be started with this 46″ (116.8 cm) area in the center of the quilt, so that the overall pattern is balanced.

   Remember that when these large areas are joined, some of the halved large and small blocks will become squares instead of triangles. The finished product will look better if some time is taken at the beginning of the project to determine where large areas are being joined and how that will affect the numbers of squares and triangles needed to mark and cut. However, if the thought of the math involved is forbidding, the large areas can be pieced separately, joining them together at the end to form the quilt top. Be warned, though, that if the latter method is chosen, visible seam lines will run through the middle of some of the squares.

2. Mark and cut all the pattern pieces, lining up the arrows on the pattern with the straight grain of the fabric and leaving seam allowances of at least ¼″ (6 mm).

   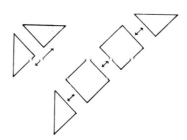

3. It's easiest to piece Irish Chain if the pattern is thought of in terms of broad diagonal rows, beginning in the top left corner. Some of these broad rows will have the large blocks in them, and some will not. Begin by piecing the small portion of the top row which is visible: piece two triangles so that they face each other and form a larger triangle. Open and press seams. Then attach, in a row, a triangle, two squares, and another triangle. Open and press seams. Sew the two rows together, and the corner has been finished.

4. Next work on the first row that contains large blocks.

   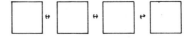

   (a) Piece four rows of four small squares each. Open and press seams.

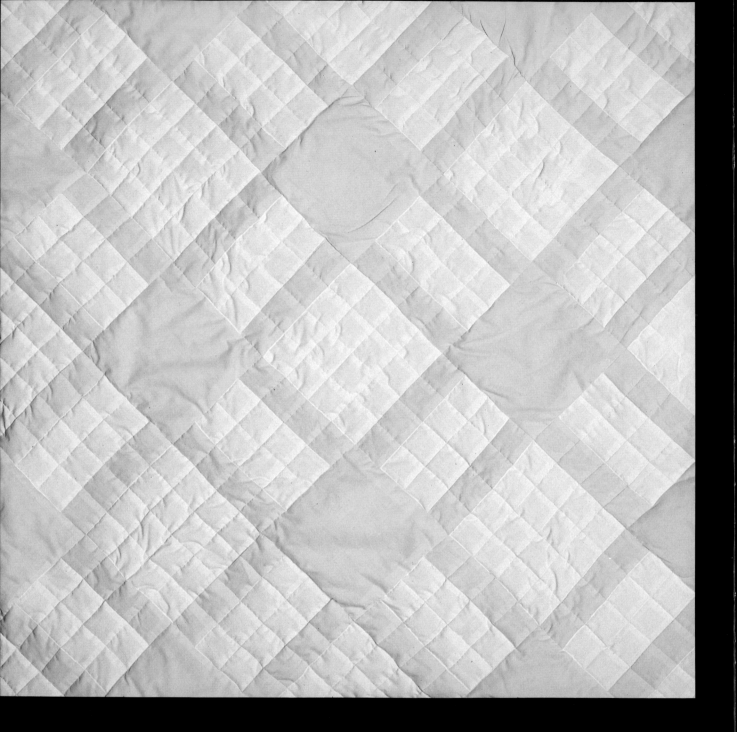

The version of Irish Chain shown in the photograph above is actually quite atypical; the use of color is more traditional. In most of the drawings (opposite) the large diamonds are noticeably separate from their background. In drawing 1 the classic design is accented by alternating rows of gray, white, and black. In 2 the colors seem to blend gently from one piece to the next, while in 3 the principal effect is one of stark contrast. Note the three-dimensional look of 4 caused by placing the darker colors toward the centers of the borders. Number 5 is a variation of a basket-weave design. Numbers 6 and 7 are similar, but the use of white in 6 accentuates the diamonds in the pattern. Number 8 and 9 take the bright colors theory to its extreme, creating a festive carnival look by using many vivid shades. Number 8 is a multicolored variation of a basket weave; and 9 is further enlivened by the pinwheels created at the intersections of each row.

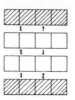

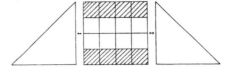

(b) Piece the rows together. Open and press seams.

(c) To each side of this sixteen-square block, add a triangle (an 8″ [20.3 cm] square halved diagonally).

5. Piece the third row, one without large blocks. First, piece three of the sixteen-square blocks described in step 4.

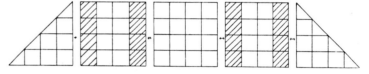

(a) Then create two large triangles from the small squares and triangles as follows: piece the bottom row (three squares and a triangle) to the next row (two squares and a triangle). Then piece those two rows to the next row (one square and one triangle). Finally, sew all three rows to the top row, a single triangle.

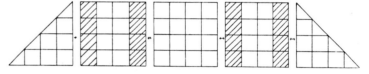

(b) Attach these two large composite triangles to the ends of the row formed by the three sixteen-square blocks. You now have the third row completed.

6. Continue in the same way, joining large blocks, halves of large blocks, sixteen-square blocks, and composite triangles to form wide diagonal rows. All four corners can be constructed as outlined in step 3.

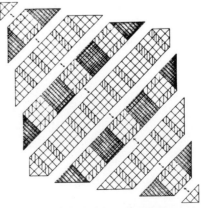

7. Sew the wide bands together to complete the quilt top or the 46″ (116.8 cm) square. Finish the quilt as outlined in the Introduction.

Pattern Pieces

Shown full size

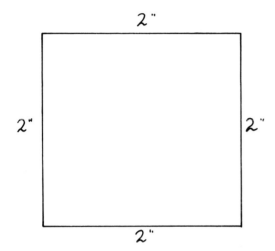

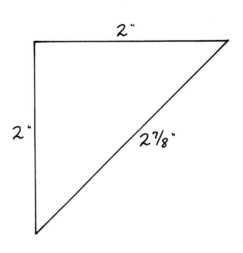

Shown half size

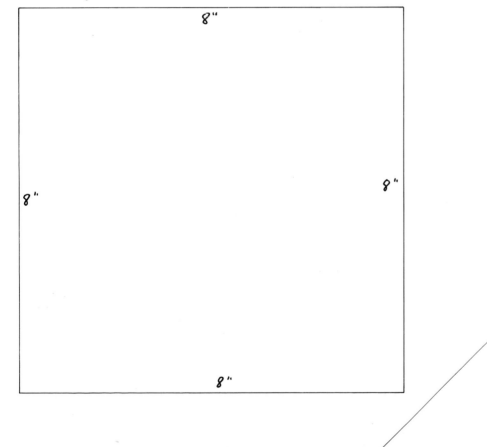

Index